Families in Children's Literature

Families in Children's Literature
A Resource Guide, Grades 4-8

Nancy Lee Cecil

Patricia L. Roberts

1998
Teacher Ideas Press
A Division of
Libraries Unlimited, Inc.
Englewood, Colorado

This one's to Chrissy for
making us a family.

Copyright © 1998 Libraries Unlimited, Inc.
All Rights Reserved
Printed in the United States of America

TEACHER IDEAS PRESS
A Division of
Libraries Unlimited, Inc.
P.O. Box 6633
Englewood, CO 80155-6633
1-800-237-6124
www.lu.com/tip

Production Editor: Kevin W. Perizzolo
Copy Editor: Jason Cook
Proofreader: Susie Sigman
Design and Layout: Pamela J. Getchell

Library of Congress Cataloging-in-Publication Data

Cecil, Nancy Lee.
  Families in children's literature : a resource guide, grades 4-8 /
Nancy Lee Cecil, Patricia L. Roberts.
    xiv, 148 p. 22x28 cm.
    ISBN 1-56308-313-2
    1. Children's literature--Study and teaching.   2. Family in
literature--Study and teaching.   I. Roberts, Patricia L., 1936-   .
II. Title.
PN1008.8.C44   1997
372.64'044--dc21   97-33635
                                                           CIP

P

Contents

Heritage and Traditions 23

Relationships Within Families 49

Conflicts Within Families 87

Introduction

The issue of family values—what they are and who has them—has been one of the most inflammatory topics in America's recent history. The questions are critical, too, for educators who daily face a heterogeneous garden of children who suddenly, it seems, come from a wide variety of families. Indeed, the children of the new millennium bring a rich background of experiential, ethnic, linguistic, and cultural backgrounds to the schoolhouse door—differences whose nuances must be recognized, appreciated, and accommodated for any instructional program to be successful. In California, for example, more than half the elementary school-age children are Hispanic, African American, or Asian. Furthermore, many children are living with one divorced parent, are getting used to new "blended" families, or are being raised by their grandparents or other relatives. Often, however, these children will not recognize *their* family, and its values and traditions, as one of those shown on television sitcoms or described in textbooks and magazine articles. Their family may contain the "traditional" mother, father, and three children, but its members are Hispanic, or of mixed races. Or another family may be white middle class but contain two caring female, adult partners and an adopted child. Yet another family may consist of a grandparent and two children of Native American descent. The face of America is definitely changing—and as it changes, so does the face of its family units.

The Changing American Family

In what other ways have the families across America changed over the last twenty years? The so-called typical American family of two parents, a father who works outside the home and a home-maker mother who raises her two or three biological children, has seen a rapid decline. According to the U.S. Census Bureau, the family has undergone a significant transition from 1970 to 1991.

Documentation of this change includes the following statistics:

- Only 26 percent of the U.S. population now consists of married different-sex couples with at least one child living at home, although 30 percent of the population includes married couples without children.
- According to the 1989 census (the most recent year for which these specific statistics are available), 27 percent of all births occurred to unwed mothers.
- The number of people living alone has increased from 20 percent in 1970 to 30 percent in 1991 (the Census Bureau considers such households "nonfamilies," even though several nonrelated individuals may be living together).
- In the most recent cases, same-sex households comprised 2 percent of the U.S. population, with children living in 5 percent of these households.
- Unmarried couples living together now number 3 million in this country, with 40 percent of these couples having children.
- Single-parent households have grown to 29 percent of all families with children. Women head 90 percent of these families.

Clearly, this rise in nontraditional domestic arrangements has led to the volatile arguments unleashed recently about family values. Some people earnestly avow that unorthodox groups of people living together are "families," while others just as adamantly disagree with this notion. While many fear that these statistics provide clear evidence that the American family is irreparably damaged, others view them more optimistically. The more optimistic view suggests that the success of a "family" might best be measured by the quality of the relationships among the people in any specific domestic arrangement and how well the family members manage their lives rather than whether or not the configuration follows the requisite pattern of mother, father, and two children (Appel 1985).

The Family, Historically and Today

The controversy surrounding family and family values may boil down to two compelling questions: What is a family? What values, if any, should every family hold? Historically, the term *family* has implied "a reciprocal sense of commitment, sharing, cooperation, and intimacy. This commitment defines the bonds between family members . . . such bonds assumed to be deeper and more lasting than those that exist in other, nonfamilial relationships" (Dizard and Gadlin 1990).

Historically, a pervasive cliché in American life has been that the family is the nucleus of the entire society; indeed, the family generally is considered to be the veritable building block for future societal relationships. This belief stems from colonial America, where all interpersonal relationships were subject to the same "guiding values and inner purposes . . . the family and the wider community [were] joined in a relation of profound reciprocity; one might almost say they [were] continuous with one another" (Demos 1986). In those days, according to historian John Demos, all values and models for behavior emanated from the family and were then reinforced synergistically by the larger community. When the community, as a part of the extended family, was replaced by a "marketplace mentality" in later years, the nuclear family assumed a place of even greater importance, where cooperation, caring, and morality could continue to flourish. In the present time, when the perpetuation of values is seen as largely the domain of the family, many people see any alternatives to the conventional nuclear family as distinctly "threatening" (Dizard and Gadlin 1990).

Today's family certainly can have a variety of configurations, as well as faces of many beautiful colors, but they should also have certain of the above-mentioned values in common. To be a family, in this author's operational definition, means to subscribe to a strong interpersonal commitment and to be willing to make sacrifices for one another. Moreover, the adults involved in a family should not only care about and support one another, but they should be present to nurture and protect children brought about by their union. Such familial goals tend to be consistent among people who differ in religion, race, wealth, and cultural heritage. Furthermore, such goals for family life are shared by people whose lifestyles may vary widely; some families may be what has been commonly referred to as traditional, while others may (if only outwardly) appear nontraditional.

Our current preoccupation with the demise of the traditional family, and our concern with family values, are nothing new. Even prior to the American War of Independence, people have taken great pride in their spirit of individualism, which places an increased emphasis on the individual person and his or her inalienable right to freedom and self-actualization; currently, it appears there is a naturally concomitant de-emphasis on family life and its obligations. Divorces and teenage pregnancies are on the rise, and there is an increased awareness about the prevalence of incest, abuse, neglect, and the abandonment of children. However, it must be noted that such ills are manifested in *all* families—traditional and nontraditional alike. Traditional families, too, as well as the most affluent and highly respected families in the public eye, are equally vulnerable to pain and debilitating dysfunction. The current spate of books telling of the disruption of families of celebrities and other public figures attest to this sobering fact.

By creating a "family curriculum," children can be guided through the confusing miasma of the rapidly changing family scene while developing a sensitivity to children living in diverse families. The cornerstone of such a family curriculum would involve introducing children to literature that has as its core main characters who live their lives as human beings from diverse races and cultures, in a wide variety of family configurations, but with universal human problems and concerns. Other literature selections might depict characters who are themselves living in traditional family settings but who demonstrate exceptional sensitivity to children living in diverse family configurations. Follow-up discussions of such literature can lead children to understand that commitment, support, and love are the most important qualities in any family, and that these qualities can be found in a variety of domestic situations, in a variety of cultures and ethnic backgrounds.

Using Children's Literature to Promote Family Concepts

Using children's literature to modify attitudes and provide insight is not new. Bibliotherapy, the use of books to help others gain additional insight and to help them cope with everyday life, is a practice dating back to the time of Aristotle, when the libraries of ancient Greece often displayed inscriptions such as "The Medicine Chest of the Soul." There is little doubt that by empathizing with believable story characters with a particular point of view, children may learn to empathize with others more sensitively. For example, when children read about a believable Asian child who lives only with his grandmother, but who appears to have the same interests, hopes, and dreams as does the reader, they are on their way to adopting a posture that emphasizes the similarities, rather than the differences, of the human condition. Moreover, the vicarious experiences involved in reading, discussing, and brainstorming tend to be much less threatening to children than real-life confrontations with unfamiliar situations. When reading, children have the luxury of reflection—they may freely explore a character's experiences and emotions—and no one sits in judgment of the reader's personal reactions.

How to Use This Book

In the following sections, teachers and librarians will find helpful activities for using children's literature as a resource to acquaint middle-school children with the myriad ways families of all races and cultures live. The activities will help children understand relationships within a family, and will offer insight into the question, What is a family?

The story summaries feature main characters who, by their actions, contribute to developing concepts about diverse families in different cultural contexts. The characters in the selected books all present positive points of view that will help promote appreciation of family diversity. Further, the characters and their stories emphasize different aspects of their family lives and their diversity. This book is divided into sections according to the primary characteristics of the families depicted: "Diverse Family Groups," "Heritage and Traditions," "Relationships Within Families," and "Conflicts Within Families." Each section is divided according to secondary family characteristics—twenty-four subsections in all, ranging from "Death in the Family" to "Homelessness."

Various literary genres are represented. Each subsection contains examples of families found in contemporary realistic fiction, folk literature, fanciful fiction, historical fiction, biographies/autobiographies, and informational text. Each book selection has a "Discussion and Beyond" section with questions to promote thoughtful reflection discussion, as well as a "Target Activity." The target activities use a variety of state-of-the-art literacy tools such as visualization, brainstorming, role plays, and creating webs to assist the teacher, parent, or librarian to help children internalize their understanding of family relationships and values.

Sharing Sensitive Issues

Many of the discussion questions and target activities in this book encourage children to respond to sensitive issues that emerge in the selected literature through fictional characters in their family settings. To facilitate sharing freely, which can be cathartic in clarifying feelings about one's family life, teachers are urged to put children in small groups, or in pairs, where they can share with a trusted friend. Additionally, it may be helpful to offer some general guidelines for student audiences; for example, students might be told that "put-downs" are never acceptable, and that there are no "right" or "wrong" family memories just as there are no "right" or "wrong" feelings. Finally, teachers are cautioned to be sensitive to the fact that oral sharing of writing and experiences can sometimes be uncomfortable, or even painful, for some students. Therefore, students should never feel pressured to share; instead, they should be told that they are always free to "pass" without any repercussions.

This text is intended to be merely a starting point for caring teachers, parents, and librarians who find themselves frustrated by the increasingly complex issues surrounding the meaning of the terms *family* and *family values*. Though even the most committed teachers and librarians cannot provide positive family role models for the children in their charge, they can offer themselves as caring role models, open to the diversity of the constellation of family groups in our society. Moreover, they can enhance family-life education by introducing quality children's literature that depicts a variety of unique families while offering carefully crafted activities that will help children acquire a new respect for the diversity of families. This is a step toward that end.

References

Appel, K. W. 1985. *America's changing families: A guide for educators.* Bloomington, IN: Phi Delta Kappa Educational Foundation.

Demos, J. 1986. *Past, present, and personal: Family life and the life course in American history.* New York: Oxford University Press.

Dizard, J. E., and H. Gadlin. 1990. *The minimal family.* Amherst, MA: University of Massachusetts Press.

Bibliography

Bernstein, J. 1983. *Books to help children cope with separation and loss.* 2d ed. New York: Bowker.

Dosch, J. 1985. *Family: Changing faces of American families.* Illustrated by K. Chenoweth-Corky. Dubuque, IA: Kendall/Hunt.

Duncan, G. J. 1993. Study: Poverty cuts kids' IQs. Paper presented at the Society for Research for Child Development, New Orleans, Louisiana, March 26.

Levitan, S., and R. Belous. 1981. *What's happening to the American family?* Baltimore, MD: Johns Hopkins University Press.

Minton, L. 1993. Fresh voices. *Parade Magazine* 4 (March 7): 20

Norton, D. 1995. *Through the eyes of a child: An introduction to children's literature.* 4th ed. New York: Macmillan.

Popenoe, D. 1988. *Disturbing the nest: Family change and decline in modern societies.* New York: Aldine De Gruyter.

Sutherland, Z., and M. H. Arbuthnot. 1986. *Children and books.* Glenview, IL: Scott, Foresman.

Takaki, R. 1993. Multicultural history lecture. Presentation at Georgetown University, Virginia, March 26.

Young, M., and P. Willmott. 1973. *The symmetrical family.* New York: Pantheon.

Diverse Family Groups

PHYSICALLY DISABLED FAMILY MEMBER

Byars, Betsy (1970). *The Summer of the Swans.* **New York: Puffin.**

Heritage: European

Family Context:

✦ family member with a physical disability

✦ absent father

✦ family support

✦ sibling relationships

Genre: contemporary realistic fiction

Grades: 4–6

Sara's fourteenth summer is turning out to be the most confusing time of her life. Before, things had flowed smoothly, and she had been happy with everyone and everything. Now, she just wants to get away from her family—her beautiful older sister, her bossy Aunt Willie with whom she lives, her remote father who does not live with them, and even herself. Her younger brother, Charlie, is mentally and physically disabled. Although she knows that she loves her brother, Sara does not realize how much until he disappears one night. That night, Sara discovers what it means to care more about someone else than yourself.

Discussion and Beyond: Family Roles

Each family member's role in family life is created by their strengths and limitations. Ask students to discuss how each of the following members of Sara's family contributed to the emotional well-being of the other family members:

- Sara
- Sara's sister
- Sara's father
- Aunt Willie
- Charlie

Target Activity: Taking Family Members for Granted

On an overhead transparency or the chalkboard, write "Taking for Granted." Ask students if they know what this means and if any of their family members have ever felt taken for granted. Discuss how Sara took Charlie for granted and sometimes even thought that he was a pest—but when he disappeared, she realized how much she loved him. Invite students to write a paragraph about a family member whom they think they have been taking for granted. Have students close the paragraph with one special thing they can do to demonstrate their love for that person.

Christopher, Matt (1995). *Fighting Tackle*. New York: Little, Brown.

Heritage: European

Family Context:

✦ family member with a physical disability

✦ family adversity

✦ sibling relationships

Genre: realistic fiction

Grades: 6–8

While this story is mainly about Terry's adjustment to his football coaches' decision to move him from defensive safety to nose tackle, the story also concerns Terry's love for his younger brother, Nicky, who was born with Down's Syndrome. Terry wants to help him become a good runner, but he is embarrassed by some of Nicky's mannerisms. When their father is injured, the brothers learn to work together instead of fighting. The reader's understanding of the term *brotherhood* is greatly expanded through this touching story.

Discussion and Beyond: Deflecting Negative Comments

Have students share how they think Terry must have felt when Nicky displayed mannerisms that seemed strange to others. Why would this bother Terry? Ask students to brainstorm some responses that Terry might have given when he heard others teasing or ridiculing his brother. How could such a situation be changed from negative to positive through patience?

Target Activity: Understanding Down's Syndrome

Using encyclopedias, CD-ROMs, trade books, and other resources, have students research Down's Syndrome. If possible, invite a guest speaker to your classroom who has a relative with this disability and can attest to the almost unlimited potential of such individuals when they are blessed with support and love. Create a classroom display of students' discoveries about Down's Syndrome and contributions individuals with this disability can make if given a chance.

de Angeli, Marguerite (1949). *The Door in the Wall.* New York: Doubleday.

Heritage: English

Family Context:

✦ family member with a physical disability

✦ family crisis

Genre: historical fiction

Grades: 6–8

When the plague strikes thirteenth-century England, Robin's noble father is off to the wars, and his mother is with the queen. When Robin falls ill and is unable to move his legs, the servants desert him. Brother Luke finds the boy and cares for him. To the despairing Robin, Luke says words from which the title of the story is taken: "Always re-member . . . thou hast only to follow the wall far enough and there will be a door in it."

Discussion and Beyond: The Caring Other as Family Member

With students, discuss the idea of the caring monks as Robin's "family" while his parents were away. Ask students to recall what the monks taught Robin; discuss specific examples, as foreshadowed by Brother Luke's words: "We must teach thy hands to be skilled in many ways, and we must teach thy mind to go about whether thy legs will carry thee or no." Discuss Brother Luke's comment "Reading is another door in the wall." Discuss the strength of Robin's spirit, which he displayed while learning to swim and using crutches, and his

heroic effort to save a beleaguered castle by escaping enemy soldiers and enlisting help at a nearby castle.

Target Activity: Encouragement from Family Members

Throughout *The Door in the Wall*, helpful sayings and advice are offered to Robin to help cope with his life. Ask students to think of a helpful saying or advice that has been given to them by a parent or caring friend or relative in their life. On 12-by-6-inch tagboard, have students write the saying or advice in bold, block print and create a design for the borders of the tagboard. Have students present the finished product to the parent or caring friend or relative as a plaque to be framed.

Bernstein, Joanne E., and Bryna Fireside (1991). *Special Parents, Special Children.* **Photographs by Michael Bernstein. New York: Albert Whitman.**

Heritage: European

Family Context:

✦ family member with a physical disability

✦ diverse families

Genre: informational text

Grades: 4–6

Angela, Adam, Lisa, and Stephanie have something in common: Each has at least one physically disabled parent. Through black-and-white photographs and straightforward text, the authors explore what it is like for these children to grow up in a family that is "special."

Discussion and Beyond: Appreciating Physical Diversity

On the chalkboard, make two columns. Label on one column "Same" and the other column "Different." Ask students to consider what areas of family life would be different if one of their parents had a physical disability. How might family life remain the same? In a family with a physically disabled parent, what traits would be especially helpful for the children to have?

Target Activity: Interviewing Someone Who Knows About "Special" Families

Invite the special education teacher from your school or another school to attend a classroom interview. Before the interview, discuss with the class questions that students have about living in a family with a physically disabled parent. Have students make a list of questions for the special education teacher. Elicit some of their questions and write them on the chalkboard. After the interview, refer to the questions and determine which questions were answered and what students have learned about the problems a special family faces.

Bawden, Nina (1975). *The Robbers.* **New York: Lippincott.**

Heritage: European

Family Context:

✦ **family member with a physical disability**

✦ **family conflict**

✦ **homelessness**

Genre: contemporary realistic fiction

Grades: 6–8

Nine-year-old Philip is new to London. His life becomes difficult when the children at school tease him about his fine manners. Darcy, an active female character, makes friends with Philip after he is teased and attacked by children at his new school. Philip's outlook changes when he makes friends with Darcy, a street child whose crippled father is a canal worker. Darcy and Philip develop a friendship, despite their differences: Darcy lacks fine manners but is independent and competent in her unprotected world; Philip has a fine lifestyle in his grandmother's apartment. Philip matures as he comes to the realization that not everyone lives in a protected environment.

Discussion and Beyond: Manners Are for Everyone

Have students enumerate problems that would arise if everyone behaved rudely. Ask students if they think that good manners are "masculine," "feminine," or "human." Invite the students to share what they know about how manners differ across cultures (e.g., in the Arabic world it is considered rude to display the bottoms of one's shoes).

Target Activity: A Family Without Sensitivity

Ask students why the children teased Philip because of his fine manners. Discuss the meaning of *elegant*, and discuss Philip's elegant manners. Have students close their eyes for a visualization activity: Ask students to imagine a family in which people have no sensitivity to the feelings of others—everyone says exactly what is on their minds; no one says "please" or "thank you" but just grabs whatever they want; no one says "excuse me" but just knocks each other down; no one is introduced to anyone, is greeted by anyone, or considers the feelings of others.

Strachan, Ian (1990). *The Flawed Glass.* Boston: Little, Brown.

Heritage: European

Family Context:

✦ family member with a physical disability

✦ family diversity

✦ family support

Genre: contemporary realistic fiction

Grades: 5–8

Shona MacLeod lives with her family on a remote island off the coast of Scotland. Because of her physical disability, which makes walking and talking difficult, Shona sees herself as flawed glass. She is sharp and clear but cannot communicate. An American family moves to the island, and she rescues the son, Carl, from a nearly fatal accident. A friendship begins between Shona and Carl—she shows him the island, and he teaches her to use the computer. After Shona witnesses a poaching incident and the poachers try to frame Shona's father, she eliminates friction between the two families, who disagree on many environmental issues. When Carl returns to America, she continues the friendship by using a modem to send and receive electronic mail.

Discussion and Beyond: When a Family Moves

With students, discuss the problems that arise when one moves from an old home to a new home, just as Carl and his family did. Discuss the new friendships that develop as well as how to maintain these friendships, just as Shona did. Ask students to make a list of their suggestions for maintaining new friendships.

Target Activity: Flawed Glass

Ask students why they think Shona may have seen herself as "flawed glass." Ask them to think of anything about themselves that makes them feel less than perfect. Encourage students to write a letter to Shona telling her what they learned about her that is good and worthwhile, and have them list what they think she should concentrate on instead of focusing on her disability. Invite students to read their letters aloud as if they were reading them to Shona.

Whelan, Gloria (1991). *Hannah.* Illustrated by Leslie Bowman. New York: Knopf.

Heritage: European

Family Context:

✦ family member with a physical disability

✦ family support

Genre: historical fiction

Grades: 5–8

In the West in 1887, nine-year-old Hannah copes with her blindness and proves that she can learn at school by listening. She discovers that she can read books in Braille. At the close of the story, the children follow the class bully's leadership and earn money to buy Hannah a Braille writer.

Discussion and Beyond: Coping Skills

Discuss with students the specific coping skills Hannah needed to deal with her blindness. Ask students how the following people could have assisted Hannah in her effort to become independent:

- her parents
- her siblings
- her extended family
- her teacher
- her friends

Target Activity: Family Members and Friends Who Help

With the students, relate the story to contemporary times and have the students point out times when they have gathered together to do something positive for a classmate—particularly one who was physically disabled. Record the information on the chalkboard or on a class chart. Ask them to divide into small groups and write a brief skit about a time from their experience when family members have gathered to do something positive for another member of the family or a friend.

STEP FAMILIES

Hopkins, Lee Bennett (1993). *Mama and Her Boys.* **Illustrated by S. Marchesi. New York: Simon & Schuster.**

Heritage: European

Family Context:

✦ stepfamilies

✦ mother-son relationship

Genre: contemporary realistic fiction

Grades: 4–6

Like marriage and adoption, remarriage requires the special consideration of all who will be affected by the change. Hopkins's story shares the importance of the relationship between a mother and her sons. Each of the sons reacts to Mama's remarriage in a different way. The story recounts the slow building of a relationship between each son and their mother's new husband. It addresses with sensitivity the many problems of remarriage. This reissued chapter book has an informative afterword in which Hopkins describes his search for and reunion with his father.

Discussion and Beyond:
A Remarriage in the Family

With the students, role play a discussion with a child whose mother or father has announced their intention to remarry. How would this child feel?

Ask the students to follow up with a brief discussion about the feelings that occur with such a change in family life. Engage the students in making decisions about what children in the family can do to help make a remarriage successful.

Target Activity:
Think, Pair, and Share

Divide the class into groups of three students each. Have each student list ways to help smooth the transition in a family changed by the introduction of remarriage and stepsiblings. Ask students to pass around their lists to share within the group, and encourage other group members to add to the lists. Have one member of each group act as recorder and collate the group's ideas. Have another member of the group act as a reporter and share the group's ideas with the rest of the class.

Boyd, Candy Dawson (1993). *Chevrolet Saturdays.* **New York: Macmillan.**

Heritage: African American

Family Context:

✦ stepfamilies

✦ divorce

✦ family conflict

Genre: contemporary realistic fiction

Grades: 5–7

Joey, an African American boy in the fifth grade, becomes self-centered when he discovers that his parents will divorce and his mother will remarry. To his mother's distress, Joey refuses to accept his stepfather and calls him Mr. Johnson. Joey's relationships at home and school suffer until his stepfather talks to the school principal. As Joey comes to regard his stepfather from a new perspective, a friendship between them begins.

Discussion and Beyond: Adjusting to a Different Lifestyle

To describe the anguish of moving away after a divorce and the pain of forming new friendships, read aloud excerpts from *There's No Surf in Cleveland* (Wilmington, MA: Clarion, 1993) by Stephanie Jona Buehler, a novel similar in theme to *Chevrolet Saturdays* in that both stories concern preadolescent boys who must move to a very different part of the country as a result of divorce and a parent's new relationship. In Los Angeles, Phillip feels an earthquake, and he notices that Santas wear sunglasses and gym shoes in the warm climate. When he cannot visit his grandparents in Cleveland over the winter holidays because his grandmother has sprained her ankle, Phillip has no choice but to take a driving trip with his mother and her boyfriend up the California coast. Other changes he faces, such as a confrontation with a bully, are resolved.

Target Activity: Give and Take

It takes compromises from all family members to make a newly-formed, "blended" family function effectively. Ask students to think of ways each family member in this story could behave to make it easier for the other family members to adjust. Have students write three short letters—one to Joey, one to his stepfather, and one to his mother—offering specific advice and strategies to make the transition easier for the others. Have students share their letters in small groups. Invite students who have experienced disrupted family relationships to offer insights as to which strategies would be the most helpful.

Pettit, Jayne (1993). *My Name Is San Ho.* **New York: Scholastic.**

Heritage: Vietnamese
Family Context:
+ stepfamilies
+ family heritage
Genre: contemporary realistic fiction
Grades: 4–6

All his days, San Ho has seen his country at war. His mother sends him from Vietnam to Saigon for his safety. A few years later, she arranges for him to join her and her new husband, an American marine, in the United States. In America, San struggles to adjust—he overcomes fears, starts school in his new country, learns English, makes new friends, faces racism, and gets acquainted with his stepfather.

Discussion and Beyond: A Case Study of San Ho

To help students understand and empathize with other young people and their family problems, discuss San Ho's problems—particularly the problem of learning to live in a new environment within a "blended" family—and his solutions to the problems, as presented in the story. Discuss alternative ways to solve these problems. Ask the students to think of the consequences of the alternatives, identify the best solutions, and support their conclusions with specific reasons. Record the problems, alternative solutions, and consequences on the chalkboard.

Target Activity: Dealing with Family Conflict

Tell students that almost every child has conflicts with family members at one time or another, but that, sometimes, others can offer objective advice. Ask students to write a "Dear Abby" letter describing a present or recent problem that they are experiencing or have experienced with a family member. Inform them that if they feel uncomfortable divulging a problem, they can create a hypothetical problem. Ask students not to sign their letter. Collect the letters, redistribute them randomly, and ask the students to write helpful responses.

COMMUNITY AS FAMILY

Levitt, Paul M., and Elissa S. Guralnick (1988). *The Stolen Appaloosa and Other Indian Stories*. Illustrated by Carolynn Roche. New York: Bookmakers Guild.

Heritage: Native American

Family Context:

✦ community as family

✦ family concerns

✦ two-parent family

Genre: folk literature

Grades: 4–6

Each story is set in a family within a community; in each case the community appears more relevant in the main character's life than the family.

This is a collection of five tales from the Native American tribes of the Pacific Northwest. In "The Story of Hot and Cold," mythic narrators tell a tale of how the seasons changed, a story reminiscent of the Greek account of Demeter and Persephone. In "The Stolen Appaloosa," a beautiful horse is the prize in a battle between two magicians who use their powers as weapons. In another tale, a woman prefers a dog to a human suitor, and is reunited with her people only when her offspring prove to be the hunters that save the village during a difficult winter. The fourth tale tells how the Indians use their magic to defeat an attempt by the white people to steal their homes. The final tale tells of the ability of the people in the community to outwit an evil bush-tailed rat man and win back their families, their livelihood, and their dignity.

Discussion and Beyond: Family Relationships in Tales from the Native American Tribes of the Pacific Northwest

With students, discuss "The Story of Hot and Cold," and ask them if they know of similar folktales about a mother's love for her daughter. Read the story of Demeter and Persephone, and discuss the similarities and differences between the two stories. Create a chart to compare family relationships in folk literature of different cultures. Display the chart so that the students can add information as they read additional stories.

Target Activity: Retelling the Stories with a Story Board

Divide the class into five groups and have each group select one of the Native American stories. Using pieces of felt and flannel, have each group create figures of the family members, friends, and other characters in their story. Using a story board covered with felt or flannel (construct by affixing a piece of felt or flannel to a 2-by-3-foot piece of sturdy cardboard), have group members retell their tale to another group in class using their flannel figures as a visual display of the action. Encourage interested groups to share their story board presentation with the entire class or with other classes at school.

Morpurgo, Michael (1991). *Waiting for Anya*. New York: Viking.

Heritage: Jewish

Family Context:

◆ community as family

◆ absent father

◆ family adversity

Genre: historical fiction

Grades: 5–8

In southern France during World War II, Jo discovers that Widow Horcada is sheltering Benjamin, her Jewish son-in-law, and is helping smuggle Jewish children across the border. Benjamin is waiting for Anya, his daughter from whom he has been separated. German soldiers are sent to occupy the village and stop refugees from escaping into Spain. Benjamin needs the help of the village to save the children. Jo devises a plan to help several Jewish children who are hiding nearby to escape into Spain. Jo and her family and friends learn that Germans are human and that there are similarities between Germans and Jews.

Discussion and Beyond: The Human Race as a Family

With older students, discuss the concept of human race as a family. Use the story of Anya and her father to help students understand and empathize with other young people and their family problems.

Discuss the problems that are presented in this story—problems caused by following (or not following) one's conscience or duty to discern right from wrong—and suggest alternative ways to cope with these problems. Ask the students to discuss how the world would benefit if everyone considered the human race to be their family. Record students' ideas on the chalkboard.

Target Activity: The Human Family

Encourage students to write a short essay about a world in which all people genuinely care about one another and display the qualities that define a family—love, support, and commitment. Ask students to imagine themselves living in such a world and to address in their essay such problems as war, crime, competition, and jealousy, and how the these problems could be altered.

Meltzer, Milton (1988). *Rescue: The Story of How Gentiles Saved Jews in the Holocaust*. New York: Harper & Row.

Heritage: European

Family Context:

◆ community as family

◆ family adversity

Genre: historical fiction

Grades: 6+

Gentiles in Europe risked their lives to save Jews from death. From archives of the Yad Vashem and libraries in New York, Meltzer has gathered together facts about the humanitarian acts of individuals and Gentiles in different countries. His exciting, true stories of the heroic and compassionate people who sought to rescue Jews from their Nazi captors create a tribute to their courage. Despite differences in their beliefs, Gentiles (at great danger to themselves) helped Jewish families persevere and escape from Nazi persecution in Europe.

Discussion and Beyond: Depending upon Others

Emphasize the point that sometimes families must depend on community members and people beyond their nuclear group to survive difficult sit-uations. Ask for volunteers who are willing to share instances when their family requested or received help from others.

Target Activity: Compassionate Heroes and Heroines Are Found in Many Families

With the students, discuss the meaning of com-passion and the qualities of heroes and heroines. Have the students contribute words related to com-passion and heroes and heroines, and list these words on the chalkboard. With further discussion, demon-strate how these words can be grouped into categories to show relationships. Reorganize the categorized words into a word web with "Compassionate Heroes and Heroines Are Found in Many Families" at the center of the diagram.

Sewall, Marcia (1990). *People of the Breaking Day.* New York: Atheneum.

Heritage: Native American

Family Context:

✦ community as family

✦ family responsibility

✦ family support

✦ intergenerational relationship

Genre: informational text

Grades: 4–5

Written in poetic prose, this book is an account of the Wampanoag Nation who lived in southeast-ern Massachusetts before the English settlers ar-rived. It portrays daily activities in the Native American community and focuses on the place of each member in Wampanoag society. Using the cycles of seasons and generational relationships as a framework, the author details how this people hunted, farmed, and survived; worked and played; and shared their beliefs, traditions, and customs.

Discussion and Beyond: Describing the People of the Breaking Day

Read aloud excerpts from the book to illustrate the poetic-prose writing of the author. Ask the stu-dents to contribute words that describe how the children, women, and men supported their families and their community. Write the words on the chalk-board, a chart, or an overhead transparency. Review the list as a class and ask students to suggest how the words can be grouped together (e.g., words about hunting, about farming, etc.). Demonstrate for the students how to transform the list of words into a web with a center circle labeled "Descriptive Words," and their ideas radiating from the center.

Target Activity: Looking More Closely at a Community

After students have learned about the different activities performed by the people in the Wampanoag community, invite them to play the roles of different members of this Native American people. Have them act as if they were living in this Native American community in the time period before English settlers arrived. Guide the role play with statements such as:

1. It is morning (afternoon, evening, night) on a spring (summer, fall, winter) day. Where are you?

2. What are you doing?

3. What are you seeing, saying, touching, hearing, and feeling?

Appoint several students to be "careful observers"—have them watch and, later, describe to the class the roles that were played.

ADOPTION

Rosen, Michael J. (1995). *Bonesy and Isabel.* **Illustrated by the author. New York: Harcourt Brace.**

Heritage: Hispanic

Family Context:

✦ adoption

✦ family heritage

✦ death of a family pet

Genre: realistic fiction

Grade: 4

This bittersweet story portrays the relationships among an adopted immigrant child from El Salvador, Isabel; her new family; and their old dog, Bonesy. The child and her dog become companions as he helps her adjust to her new life in a foreign country with strange people and no common language. When Bonesy dies, Isabel finds that she shares grief with her new family, who loved the old dog as much as she did. Isabel realizes that she does not need words to communicate—tears alone express her feelings. Vivid oil paintings capture the story's mood.

Discussion and Beyond: The Importance of Pets

Ask students for a show of hands for those who have ever had a family pet. Encourage students to share how pets can be important members of the family. Offer the idea that if a pet dies, it can be as heart-wrenching as losing a member of the family. Ask those students who have experienced such a loss, and who are willing, to share in small groups how their feelings of loss were similar to Isabel's feelings.

Target Activity: Other Forms of Communication

The first time Isabel really communicated with her new family was when Bonesy died and she felt bonded by their mutual grief. Brainstorm other universal forms of communication that human beings use to share feelings with one another, such as music, dancing, laughter, and facial gestures. Invite students to act out these communications as they might do if they were attempting to befriend Isabel.

Wright, Richard (1984). *Rite of Passage.* **New York: HarperCollins.**

Heritage: European

Family Context:

✦ adoption

✦ community as family

✦ family conflict

✦ intergenerational relationship

Genre: contemporary realistic fiction

Grades: 6–8

Wright's novella examines the situation of a young boy who has grown up in Harlem. Richard, at age fifteen, runs away from his foster home only to become involved with a gang of angry, violent juvenile delinquents whom he begins to think of as his family.

Discussion and Beyond: Peers in a Gang as Family

Ask students if they have ever confided in a peer in a way that they would not have confided to members of their family or foster family. Discuss how confiding in peers is a normal thing to do as one grows older. Discuss the value of a peer confidant as well as the danger in becoming involved with gang members who are violent and angry:

1. Do you know anyone who has become involved with teenage gang members who are angry and violent?

2. What changed for Richard when he became involved with a gang?

3. If you were with Richard, living in Harlem, what would you do to help him realize the value of a home and the danger of becoming involved with violent gang members?

4. What would you do to help Richard face the anger and violence of others?

Target Activity: An Upsetting Incident

After discussion, ask the students to write a paragraph about a time when an occurrence in their family or foster home upset them. Encourage students to develop in the paragraph a conversation that they had with a peer about the incident. Have students close the paragraph with a few sentences that reveal how they felt after sharing their problem with someone their age.

Byars, Betsy (1979). *The Pinballs.* **New York: Scholastic.**

Heritage: European

Family Context:

✦ adoption

✦ family support

Genre: contemporary realistic fiction

Grades: 5–8

Brought together under the same roof, three foster children prove to each other and to the world that they are a family. They also prove that they are not pinballs to be knocked around from one place to the next—they have a choice in life: to try or not to try. The children overcome many obstacles through their perseverance and their commitment to one another. The author has taken what could have been a sad story and turned it into a hopeful and humorous book.

Discussion and Beyond: Obstacle or Challenge?

Make two columns on the chalkboard or on an overhead transparency. Label one "Obstacle" and the other "Challenge." Ask students to think of a hardship that they have faced in their life. Ask them to decide if it was an obstacle or a challenge. Have students describe how a family member, through support and encouragement, helped them see that what seemed like an obstacle could become a worthwhile challenge. Offer personal examples to initiate the discussion.

Target Activity: If at First You Don't Succeed . . .

Ask students to write a short paragraph about a time when they tried to do something and it seemed too difficult, much like the "pinball" children.

Encourage them to share how their perseverance paid off and how their family's love and support helped them succeed. Create a "If at First You Don't Succeed" bulletin board to display students' writing.

Christopher, Matt (1995). *Double Play at Shortstop.* **New York: Little, Brown.**

Heritage: European

Family Context:

✦ adoption

Genre: realistic fiction

Grades: 4–6

Danny, an adopted twelve-year-old, plays as hard as he can in the baseball championship series. He has a good chance of being chosen for the all-star team, but he becomes distracted by the opposing team's shortstop. Why is he so interested in her? Why does she watch him so carefully? As the plot unfolds, Danny learns that she is his twin sister, who was adopted at birth by another family.

Discussion and Beyond: Seeing Your Twin

It is commonly said that everyone on the planet has a twin somewhere, and many people have had the experience of someone telling them that they look exactly like someone else they know. Ask students if they have ever had this experience and

how it felt. How must Danny have felt seeing his female counterpart when he knew he had a twin sister somewhere? Ask students what they might have done in a similar situation.

Target Activity: Comparing Two Plots

Rent the Walt Disney video *The Parent Trap* from your local video store. Show students the ten-to fifteen-minute excerpt in which the twin girls meet at camp and realize that they are practically mirror images of each other. Using a comparison chart have students compare the reactions of the twins in the book and the twins in the video. Encourage students to help you make a list on the chalkboard of the possible positive and negative feelings that might be associated with finding a sibling you were not aware you had.

Bennett, James (1994). *Dakota Dream*. New York: Scholastic.

Heritage: Native American

Family Context:

✦ adoption/new family

✦ family conflict

✦ family traditions

Genre: contemporary realistic fiction

Grades: 6–8

A foster home is the only family that Floyd Rayfield—also known as Charly Black Crow—has ever known. The authorities in his group home are insensitive and do not understand that Charly is searching for his vision as a future Dakota warrior (they believe that he needs help from a psychiatrist). To fulfill his vision, Charly leaves the group home and goes to the Dakota reservation to convince the chief that he can become a sincere member of the tribe (his new family). He submits to a ritual of fasting and undertakes his vision quest. He completes his rituals satisfactorily, and from his vision quest he gains insight about the authorities he faced in his foster home.

Discussion and Beyond: What Sensitivities Do Family Members Need?

Sometimes, family members are insensitive to the feelings of another and do not understand the ambitions and interests that drive another's self-fulfillment. With the students, discuss this contemporary story and the determination of Charly to be a future Dakota warrior with an "adopted" family of acquaintances on the Dakota reservation. Read and discuss any words or phrases from the story that express the need for a person from any family— foster home or other family arrangement—to search for one's vision.

Target Activity: Adjusting to New Family Traditions

Ask students if there are any traditions or rituals in their families that outsiders might find confusing or even unsettling. Have students write a persuasive speech trying to convince the outsider, as Charly had to convince the authorities, that the tradition or ritual has meaning for them and should be respected.

Lee, Marie G. (1993). *If It Hadn't Been for Yoon Jun*. Boston: Houghton Mifflin.

Heritage: Korean

Family Context:

✦ adoption

✦ family support

Genre: contemporary realistic fiction

Grades: 6–8

Alice Larson is starting seventh grade, and her interests center around cheerleading, her two closest friends, and football hero Troy Hill. Though she feels as American as her adoptive parents and their biological daughter, who are of Norwegian descent, she is constantly reminded of her Korean heritage. When her adoptive father, a minister, asks her to befriend the new Korean students at her school, Alice balks at the idea. Yoon Jun Lee, a Korean student, is pudgy, has acne, does not speak much English, and seems "different." When Alice and Yoon Jun are paired up to do a report on Korea, Alice discovers that she can learn much through her friendship with Yoon Jun, and she begins to understand that her Korean heritage actually means something to her. Though the plot is somewhat predictable, this book will be of great interest to Korean adoptees and to children living in a family with siblings who are Korean adoptees because of its theme—a nurturing, multicultural family relationship.

Discussion and Beyond: Learning About Our Heritage

If it hadn't been for her friendship with Yoon Jun Lee, Alice might never have learned so much about Korea. What might her life have been like without this knowledge? If it hadn't been for Yoon Jun, Alice might never have discovered that her Korean heritage could actually mean something to her. Ask students how they knew that Alice had begun to understand that her Korean heritage actually meant something to her.

Target Activity: If It Hadn't Been For . . .

To help students understand and empathize with Korean adoptees and with children living in a family with siblings who are Korean adoptees, discuss the problems presented in the story, as Alice sees them, as well as several ways that Alice might have coped with them. Ask the students to identify Alice's problems, the coping skills Alice might have used, and any consequences of the coping strategies. Ask students to support their conclusions with specific reasons.

GAY FAMILY MEMBER

Heron, Ann, and Meredith Maran (1991). *How Would You Feel If Your Dad Was Gay?* **Illustrated by Kris Kovick. Boston: Alyson Wonderland.**

Heritage: European

Family Context:

♦ gay parent

♦ diverse family

♦ family concerns

Genre: contemporary realistic fiction

Grades: 4–6

Michael, Jasmine, and Noah are average kids, except for one thing—they each have gay parents. They have unique concerns, concerns that do not seem to affect the lives of any of their friends, such as dealing with name calling that is directed at their parents as well as them. The three children are ashamed of their parents until a very sensitive teacher develops an assembly program for the school dealing with many different kinds of families whose members are committed to one another.

This book, written by two lesbian mothers with help from their sons, will be most significant for other young people who are facing the same issues. It may also help the classmates, parents, librarians, and teachers of these students better understand just how varied today's families can be.

Discussion and Beyond:
Further Interest in Reading About Homosexuality

For those students interested in reading more about the subject, suggest *Know About Gays and Lesbians* (Highland Park, NJ: Millbrook, 1994) by Margaret O. Hyde and Elizabeth H. Forsyth, an information book for grades 6+ that traces a detailed history of same-sex relationships from ancient times to contemporary times. The text addresses such milestones as the decision of the American Psychiatric Association to remove homosexuality from the list of mental illnesses in 1973, the decriminalization of homosexuality state by state, and the growing number of businesses and state and local governments that now provide benefits to homosexual partners. Have interested students report back on the book and open up the topic for discussion.

Target Activity:
Facing Verbal Abuse

Ask students if they have ever been the victims of name calling, for any reason. Is it ever right to call someone hurtful names? Have small groups of students role play scenarios in which they offer positive responses to name-callers.

Fox, Paula (1996). *The Eagle Kite.* **New York: Orchard Press.**

Heritage: European

Family Context:

✦ gay family member

✦ death

✦ father-son relationship

Genre: realistic fiction

Grades: 7–8

The truth has haunted Liam for three years, yet he feels he has to keep the truth to himself: His father has AIDS. This is a poignant story for mature readers that deals frankly with the issues of AIDS, death, prejudice, and the difficulties for a young boy trying to grow up in today's world.

Discussion and Beyond: Defending a Parent

Ask students to share how they think Liam must have felt when almost everyone turned away from his father at a time when he most needed support. How might Liam have best responded to the ignorance of insensitive people? Encourage students to share incidents when the actions or words of their parents were misunderstood. How did the students respond to the accusations?

Target Activity: AIDS Awareness

Invite a guest speaker from a local health awareness facility to speak to your class about AIDS, how it is and is not transmitted, and appropriate behavior toward someone who has the disease. Have students prepare a list of questions to ask the speaker so that any fears or misconceptions can be discussed and perhaps laid to rest.

Jenness, Aylette (1990). *Families: A Celebration of Diversity, Commitment, and Love.* **New York: Harper & Row.**

Heritage: European

Family Context:

✦ gay parent

✦ divorce

✦ family diversity

✦ stepfamilies

Genre: informational text

Grades: 4–6

The lives of seventeen children and their families are described in a series of stories (one about each family) illustrated with black-and-white photographs. The text includes descriptions of the family types as well as quotations from the children and sometimes other family members. Attention is focused on what makes each family unique and how the children and their family members feel about their situation. Comments are straight-forward and deal with a variety of emotions and concerns. The family types depicted include adopted children, stepfamilies, divorced parents, gay-lesbian parents, foster siblings, multigenerational families, physically disabled parents, bilingual families, and others. Many ethnicities and cultures are represented. The book begins with multiple views from the children concerning the definition of family and closes with remarks on how people function within families.

Discussion and Beyond: What Is a Family?

Ask students to recall the diverse types of families mentioned in the book. Where there any that surprised them or that they did not consider appropriate as families? Ask students to list the attributes that are essential to a family unit. Have each student share one idea until repetition begins to occur. Describe each of the seventeen families in the book, and ask students if the attributes they listed seem to apply. Invite students to share with the class how their definition of a family has changed after reading this book.

Target Activity: How a Family Understands a Child

Ask the students to develop a story about different ways a family shows that it understands a child. Have students imagine that they are a child in a family setting that is different from theirs. Encourage students to cut out pictures from various magazines that depict life in the imagined family setting. Give the students long sections of fold-out shelf paper (or mural or newsprint paper), and have them arrange the pictures in a sequence along the paper to show the family's activities in their story. Have students write their story beneath the pictures, based on the actions shown in the pictures. Finally, have students paste down the pictures.

Heritage and Traditions

INTERGENERATIONAL RELATIONSHIPS

Koertge, Ron (1994). *Tiger, Tiger, Burning Bright*. New York: Orchard.

Heritage: European

Family Context:

✦ intergenerational relationship

✦ family problem solving

✦ family support

Genre: contemporary realistic fiction

Grades: 7–8

Thirteen-year-old Jesse is sad because his much loved grandfather, Pappy, is slipping into senility. One time, Pappy nearly burned down the house when he got excited about "seeing" tiger tracks in the nearby desert. Jesse starts covering up for Pappy so his mother won't talk anymore about a nursing home for his grandfather. At the book's end, all agree to look out for Pappy and to be a little more careful in their caretaking of Pappy.

Discussion and Beyond: Looking Out for a Family Member

With the students, discuss the idea that the members of a family can look out for an elderly member. Ask them to think of a time when someone in their family took good care of an elderly relative or friend. In what way did the elderly person show their appreciation? Invite the students to write quietly and reflectively in their journals about something they would be willing to promise to do to help care for an elderly family member.

Target Activity: Family Problem Solving

Ask students to think of a recent problem that their family experienced. Encourage them to write a paragraph about how the family solved the problem, how each family member contributed to the solution, and the outcome. Ask them to summarize their paragraph by telling how problem solving was useful to the situation. Invite the students to share their paragraphs in small groups or, for students who are willing, with the class.

Bunting, Eve (1991). *The Wall.* **Illustrated by Ronald Himler. New York: Clarion.**

Heritage: European

Family Context:

✦ intergenerational relationship

✦ family support

Genre: contemporary realistic fiction

Grades: 4–5

A boy, who has never known his grandfather, wishes his grandfather were still here while he watches another grandfather and grandson together. The boy and his father search for the name of the boy's grandfather on the memorial wall. This story can support a comparison study about feelings of family members who have suffered a loss caused by the ravages of war.

Discussion and Beyond: Wishing You Were Here

Poll students to find out how many have a grandparent they have never known. What would they like that relative to know about them and their life? What kinds of things do they wish they could have shared with that grandparent? Pair students together, and have them share with their partner a conversation they would like to have with their grandparent if they could meet them and speak with them for a few moments.

Target Activity: How Can Students Learn About a Relative They Have Never Known?

Encourage students to gather memorabilia (photographs, pictures, drawings, letters, etc.) for a deceased relative with the help of family members and friends. Encourage students to read aloud the letters and discuss the photographs, pictures, and drawings with members of the family. If desired, invite students to create a written memorial—by describing the photographs and the events in the life of the relative—to display in a prominent place in the home.

Conrad, Pam (1989). *My Daniel.* **New York: Harper & Row.**

Heritage: European

Family Context:

✦ intergenerational relationship

✦ death in the family

Genre: contemporary realistic fiction

Grades: 4–8

Eighty-year-old Julia Creath Summerwaite takes her grandchildren to the Natural History Museum in New York to see the dinosaur exhibit. She tells them about her relationship with their Great-Uncle Daniel, her brother, who died while very young. Daniel had a passion for fossils and competed fiercely with other paleontologists to find "treasures" in Nebraska.

Discussion and Beyond: Family Stories

Review the story that Julia Summerwaite told to her grandchildren and ask students if they have heard treasured stories about their family's history from a grandparent. If students cannot recall any stories, have them write to, call, or visit a grandparent, if possible, and ask to hear stories about their family's history. Have students share their stories in class.

Target Activity: What Are the Occupations of Older Family Members?

Have students research different occupations of family members and share with the class interesting discoveries. Additionally, invite students to look through the yellow pages of the regional telephone directory to identify familiar and unfamiliar occupations that interest them. Have students tell the class about the occupations that most interest them.

Fleischman, Paul (1991). *The Borning Room*. New York: HarperCollins.

Heritage: European

Family Context:

✦ intergenerational relationship

✦ family heritage

Genre: historical fiction

Grades: 6–8

This is a story about four generations of Ohioans whose most important events—births and deaths—take place in the home's "borning room." Georgina Caroline Lott, who was born there in 1851, tells the story of her family to a painter who has been hired to paint her portrait as she approaches the end of her life, which occurred in 1918.

Discussion and Beyond: A Special Room

Discuss with students how Georgina and her family must have felt about their family home, in general, and the "borning room" in particular. Ask if there are any students in the class who have lived in the same house for many years or even for several generations. Ask these students to share stories about the house or sentimental feelings about certain rooms in the house.

Target Activity: A Family Timeline

Read aloud excerpts from the story. Pair students together, and hand out index cards to each group. Have students write one sentence on each card describing an event that happened in the family life of Georgina Caroline Lott. As a class, ask each group to read aloud the sentences while two volunteers place the index cards on the chalk rail under chronological dates of a family timeline written on the chalkboard by another student or the teacher. The timeline might begin with Georgina Caroline Lott's year of birth, 1851, and end with the year of her death, 1918. Events in the history might include Lott's discovery of a runaway slave who helps her mother give birth, a deathwatch for her beloved grandfather, the loss of her mother during a subsequent childbirth, the nursing of two brothers ill with diphtheria, her marriage to the local school teacher, and the births of her children.

Taylor, Mildred (1989). *Song of the Trees.* **New York: Bantam.**

Heritage: African American

Family Context:

✦ intergenerational relationship

✦ absent father

✦ family adversity

Genre: historical fiction

Grades: 4–6

Eight-year-old Cassie and her family struggle to survive in the South during the Great Depression. To support the family, the father, David Logan, leaves their home in Mississippi to work on the railroad in Louisiana. The rest of the family—Mama, Big Ma (Cassie's grandmother), Christopher-John, Little Man, and Stacey—are left alone. With their father away, Mr. Anderson, a white man sent to chop down designated trees, offers Big Ma sixty-five dollars for the trees on the property, but she agrees only when he threatens to harm the family. The family loves the trees—the children to play around and in them and listen to the soft swoosh that is their song. The children try to stop the lumbermen from cutting down the trees and get into a scuffle with Mr. Anderson and the other lumbermen. Mr. Anderson has his belt out to strike one of the children and Father arrives and rescues the children from him. He plants dynamite in the forest and says he will blow it up if any more trees are taken. When the lumbermen leave, Father calls out, "Dear, dear old trees, will you ever sing again?" but the trees give no answer.

Discussion and Beyond: Family Survival in the Great Depression

Ask students to recount the ways that life was very difficult for Cassie and her family during the Great Depression. In what ways did this struggle bring the family closer together? In what ways did extended families help rear children during this difficult time? Will having lots of money necessarily make a family happier? Why? Invite an individual who lived during the Great Depression to speak to the class. Ask him or her to specifically address how the family coped with typical concerns during that difficult time.

Target Activity: Different Families in Different Environments

From discarded newspapers and magazines, have students cut pictures, words, and phrases that show or describe ways families live in environments suitable for the growth of trees. Ask students to discuss the pictures, words, and phrases they have selected, and engage them in designing a class mural or individual collages depicting the families and environments. Display the mural and collages in a prominent location in the school.

Douty, Esther M. (1971). *Charlotte Forten: Free Black Teacher.* **Champaign, IL: Gerrard.**

Heritage: African American

Family Context:

✦ intergenerational relationships

Genre: historical fiction

Grades: 6–8

This is a fictionalized biography of Charlotte Forten, an African American from Massachusetts. Born in the North in 1837, before the Civil War and the freeing of the slaves in the South, she was fortunate to be part of a free black family. Charlotte was most impressed with escaped slaves she met who were hidden by her family and their friends. Because the schools where she grew up after her mother's death were segregated, Charlotte was, for the most part, educated at home by her aunt. Because she had no schoolmates to talk to, she read and wrote in a journal. She also attended meetings of the Female Antislavery Society with her aunt. By the time she was eighteen, Charlotte was a teacher. She continued to write in her journal throughout her life because she wanted people to know and remember the stories of heroic slaves who fought for their freedom and the friends who helped them in their fight.

Discussion and Beyond:
Keeping a Journal

Discuss with the students how Charlotte Forten's journal writing helped her remember the struggles of her family and the people she saw around her. Ask students to keep a journal of events in their family life as well as what they think, read, and see that they might want to remember later. These events could be as ordinary as a description of a game with friends, a party at school, how a family problem was solved, a good book they read, or an idea they would like to remember.

Target Activity:
Stories from the Past

Have the students interview an adult family member or friend about their childhood and how it was different from the lives of their friends. How did living in a diverse family group make them more sensitive to others? Did it make them stronger emotionally? Did it make them more open to the problems of others? Have students write and illustrate a story about this person to share with them. Invite students to read their story to the class.

Greenfield, Eloise (1989). *Nathaniel Talking.* **Illustrated by Jan Spivey Gilchrist. New York: Writers & Readers.**

Heritage: African American

Family Context:

◆ **intergenerational relationship**

Genre: biography

Grades: 4–5

This is an account of a nine-year-old black child who presents biographical information through first-person poems about himself, his world, his memories, and his future. As part of his memories, Nathaniel pays tribute to each generation of his family through a musical form associated with their time period. For example, in "Grandfather Bones," the words and rhythm remind one of African folk instruments; in "My Daddy," the words and rhythm remind one of the blues; and in "Nathaniel's Rap," written for his generation, the words create a rap rhythm: "I can rap/I can rap/I can rap rap rap/Till your earflaps flap."

Discussion and Beyond: Tribute to Someone in the Family

Invite the students to think about the things they have done during the week to pay tribute to someone in their family. What events can they recall where they paid tribute to someone in the family? Discuss what situations students were in that now causes them to think:

1. I should have . . .

2. If only I had not . . .

3. I am glad that I . . .

Target Activity: Family Rap Song

Have students chant selected lines from Nathaniel's Rap several times. Using the lyrical and rhythmical format of that rap song, invite the students to write a rap tribute to family members, especially parents or grandparents or other extended family members. Encourage students to share their rap tribute with the class.

Reeder, Carolyn (1991). *Grandpa's Mountain*. New York: Macmillan.

Heritage: European

Family Context:

◆ intergenerational relationship

◆ family adversity

Genre: historical fiction

Grades: 5–8

Eleven-year-old Carrie visits her grandparents' home in the Blue Ridge Mountains in the summers. One summer, she finds Grandpa fighting the government men who wish to create a national park on the land. Grandpa becomes as hard and intractable as the men he opposes, a behavior that shocks Carrie. A series of events and consequences during the Great Depression has relevance for situations today in which the government still pits projected benefits for the many against total disruption for the few.

Discussion and Beyond: Considering Carrie's Life and Relationships

Ask student to respond to the following discussion questions:

1. Why did her grandfather's behavior shock Carrie? What effect did this have on their relationship?

2. What was it like for a family living in the mountains? How would such a life differ from your family life?

3. If you were a friend of Carrie's and her Grandpa during this time, what would you have done to help them? Would you have gotten involved? Why?

Target Activity: Grandpa's Mountain Neighborhood

Engage students in an activity to help them understand the problems of living in Grandpa's particular neighborhood. Divide the students into groups to represent families who live in the Blue Ridge Mountains. Give each group an index card upon which to describe the family's situation (lifestyles, jobs, incomes, and feelings about the government wanting to create a national park on their land). Have the groups trade cards and role play family situations. Ask the groups to compare their family's situation with the situations of other groups as well as with the situations of families who lived in other regions during the time of this story.

FAMILY TRADITIONS

Osborne, Chester (1984). *The Memory String.* **New York: Atheneum.**

Heritage: Native American
Family Context:
✦ family traditions
✦ family support
✦ intergenerational relationship
Genre: historical fiction
Grades: 5–7

Living on the Siberian peninsula with his people, Darath wants to be a great hunter like his father, but the tribe wants him to be a shaman, just as his grandfather was. Studying a shaman's ways, Darath learns to use Moon Sticks to keep track of time, to understand numbers, to heal with medicines, and to tell stories with the Memory String that keeps the people's history. With his sister's help, Darath finds a way for his people to cross the land bridge that joined Asia and North America at that time.

Discussion and Beyond: Following in Someone's Footsteps

With students, discuss the idea of "following in someone's footsteps." Ask students why this idea is important to some families. Ask students to think of family members who have followed in the footsteps of relatives. From their discussion, have them state why they would or would not follow in the footsteps of a family member. As a class, discuss situations in which it would be better to "do one's own thing" rather than "follow in someone else's footsteps."

Target Activity: A Model Relative

After engaging students in the discussion above, ask them to write an essay describing a relative in whose footsteps they wish to follow. Have them include the following points:

1. A description of the relative and their admirable qualities.

2. How the relative has influenced the student.

3. In what ways the student hopes to be like the relative.

4. Why the relative would be an ideal role model for others.

After revising the essays using peer editors, have students write their final draft on plain white paper and mount it on colored tagboard. Create a bulletin board display of the essays and invite the "model relatives" to come to the classroom to see their special tributes.

Ho, Minfong (1990). *Rice Without Rain.* **New York: Lothrop, Lee & Shepard.**

Heritage: Vietnamese
Family Context:
✦ family traditions
✦ community as family

Genre: historical fiction

Grades: 6+

Sri, Ned, and other Thammasart University students from Bangkok are given permission to stay in Jinda's Maekung village for a few months by Jinda's father, Inthorn, who is head of the village. Sri treats the villagers with modern medicines, and Ned helps harvest the rice. Later, Ned gets the farmers to agree to a rent resistance boycott (half of the rice crop goes to landlords for rent), but with disastrous results—Inthorn is taken to jail, and Jinda becomes torn between revolution and keeping traditions. Traveling back to Bangkok to meet again with Ned and Sri, Jinda sees a violent attack on the students' demonstration at the university (an actual event, which happened October 6, 1976) and realizes that she will have to make difficult choices about the direction of her life.

Discussion and Beyond: "Current Events Affect Family Life"

Related to the event that happened October 6, 1976, at the university in Bangkok, discuss with students the book's foreword, written by Jiranan Prasertkul, who was a leader of the demonstration and who, later, became a communist guerrilla living in the northern jungle of Thailand. Pair students together and discuss the effects of the demonstration on families—particularly the effects on Prasertkul and his family, who had to leave the university in Bangkok for the northern jungle region. Have students relate this story to a current event and suggest possible effects of the event on the families involved.

Target Activity: Cultures and Their Traditions

Have students read newspapers and periodicals for information about current revolutions and political unrest in the world. Have them research both sides of a particular issue. Ask students to write a short story, similar to *Rice Without Rain*, in which the revolution goes against the established traditions in the country. Have students conclude the story with an effective compromise—resolving the problem while respecting tradition, yet providing needed changes.

Grifalconi, Ann (1986). *The Village of Round and Square Houses.* Illustrated by the author. Boston: Little, Brown.

Heritage: African American

Family Context:

+ family traditions
+ intergenerational relationship

Genre: folk literature

Grades: 4–6

This story tells why the men in a Cameroon village, Tos, in central Africa live in square houses while the women live in round houses. One night long ago, the old Naka mountain volcano erupted and left only two houses standing in the village— one round and one square. To take care of the people while the village was being rebuilt, the village chief sent the tall men to live in the square house and the women to live in the round house. The teller of this tale says that this arrangement is peaceful and continues to this day because people need a time to be apart as much as a time to be together. The women decided that they enjoyed being together to talk, laugh, and sing in the round houses, and the men became used to relaxing in a place of their own in the square houses.

Discussion and Beyond: Families Vary According to Their Culture

With students, discuss this intergenerational Cameroon family and their cultural diversity. Help the students recognize the similarities and differences in families of different cultures. Citing examples from the story, discuss how culture is learned and how human behavior varies from group to group. Discuss the structure of the extended Cameroon family, the roles of family members, and the social functions of the family. What seems to be the main function of the family? What basic needs must the family satisfy? How does the

family satisfy their needs? What are the characteristics of the environment of this family? What web can be drawn by the students to show these environmental characteristics?

Target Activity: Storytelling in Families

Introduce Grandmother's storytelling beginning—"In the days of long, long ago"—and ending—"And that is how our way came about and why it will continue." Pair students together and have each partner tell the other a story that has been told to them by a grandmother, aunt, or other extended family member. Have students begin the story with the words "In the days of long, long ago" and end the story with "And that is how our way came about and why it will continue."

Flora, James (1994). *The Fabulous Fireworks Family.* **New York: McElderry/Macmillan.**

Heritage: Hispanic

Family Context:

◆ family traditions

◆ family problem solving

◆ sibling relationship

Genre: contemporary realistic fiction

Grades: 4–5

In the village of Santiago, Pepito and his sister Amelia live with their parents. The family is well known for their ability to create the finest pyrotechnic displays in all of Mexico. When the day of celebration for the patron saint of their village draws near, the family is called upon by the village's dignitaries to create the largest, noisiest, and most colorful fireworks castillo ever. Discussion of the history of fireworks in celebrations in Mexico is included.

Discussion and Beyond: Some Families Are Well Known Because . . .

Pepito and Amelia's family were called upon for their skills in creating fine fireworks displays. Students' families (or family members) are called upon for their skills, too. Ask students to share the skills for which their family members are known (e.g., a father who is a surgeon, an uncle who is an earthquake engineer, a brother who is a utility worker, a sister who is a police deputy, a mother who is a dentist). Make a list for the class bulletin board in recognition of the contributions of the students' family members.

Target Activity: Things We Do as a Family

Write the word *tradition* on the chalkboard, and ask students to contribute examples of what a tradition might be. Explain that such an activity need not be as exotic as making fireworks together, but it should be an activity that all family members share on a routine basis. Have students, working with partners, list the activities they engage in as traditions in their family. Ask them to select the one tradition that means the most to them and prepare a short summary of the activity and its significance to their family. Have students share their summary with the rest of the class.

FAMILY HERITAGE

Regguinti, G. (1992). *The Sacred Harvest: Ojibway Wild Rice Gathering.* **New York: Lerner.**

Heritage: Native American

Family Context:

◆ family heritage

◆ two-parent family

Genre: informational text

Grades: 4–6

Glenn Jackson, a Native American boy, is old enough to participate in a wild rice gathering to get the sacred food of his people. In the northwestern areas of the United States (and along the edges of lakes in Canada), wild rice grows in lagoons and other watery areas. The Ojibway harvest the tall grassy stalks and long black grains of wild rice from these areas. In the fall, the rice can often be harvested daily because the rice is at its growth peak and the seeds ripen continuously. The rice is stacked and dried, then threshed (the rice heads are separated from the stalks). This unhusked rice is stored for family use, and quantities are cleaned (the husks are removed) as needed. The husks are pounded off in stone mortars, or flailed or ground off between stones.

Discussion and Beyond: Participating in a Special Gathering Event

Ask students to take a few minutes and reflect upon any special gathering events that their family participates in, just as Glenn Jackson took part in a wild rice gathering to get the special food that has long been sacred to his people. A current gathering event that families might participate in would be the birth of a baby, or a family reunion, or a family member's child's high school graduation.

Invite students to describe their family's special gathering events and why the events are important to their family. Record the special events in a list on the chalkboard so students will be aware of the variety of events that have special meaning for those in the class.

Target Activity: Change and Its Effect on Families

Ask students to interview an older family member—such as a grandparent, great-aunt, or great-uncle—to discover how family life and special events that their family cherishes have changed since the relative was a child. Have students focus on the following questions:

1. What special gathering events of special significance did your extended family engage in?

2. Did both parents participate in these gatherings?

3. What were the responsibilities of each family member? How were these responsibilities different than the responsibilities of your extended family members today?

4. How were meal times different?

5. What hardships did family members endure?

Wolf, Bernard (1994). *Beneath the Stone: A Mexican Zapotec Tale.* **Photographs by the author. New York: Orchard.**

Heritage: Hispanic

Family Context:

✦ family heritage

✦ two-parent family

Genre: contemporary realistic fiction

Grades: 4–6

This story about the Zapotec family of six-year-old Vicente Golan Ruiz, is set in a village with a name and history more than 3,000 years old—Teotitlan del Valle (Beneath the Stone in the Valley). The Ruiz family members buy food and cook meals, and Vicente goes to school. They weave tapetes (tapestries—wall hangings and rugs) and sell them in Oaxaca City. They celebrate Los Dias de los Muertos (the Day of the Dead), the anniversary of the Mexican Revolution, and Christmas. This book, illustrated with full-color photographs, addresses the blending of cultural traditions from the early Zapotec people and the Spanish conquistadors and emphasizes the importance of family, community, and heritage in Vicente's life.

Discussion and Beyond: Importance of Family, Community, and Heritage

Elicit from students their thoughts about the importance of family, community, and heritage to the Ruiz family in contrast to the importance of family, community, and heritage to their family. What things are said and done in their family, and in families they know, that show the importance of family, community, and heritage to family members?

Target Activity: Family Cultural Traditions

Read aloud Diane Boyt-Goldsmith's book (for grades 4–6) *Day of the Dead: A Mexican-American Celebration* (New York: Holiday House, 1994). Mexican American twins narrate their family's activities as they prepare to observe the Day of the Dead. The family-centered celebration is shown in full-color photographs. Have students take notes, while they listen to the story, about the activities of this celebration that interest them most.

Say, Allen (1993). *Grandfather's Journey.* **Illustrated by the author. Boston: Houghton Mifflin.**

Heritage: Japanese

Family Context:

✦ family heritage

✦ family traditions

✦ intergenerational relationship

Genre: historical fiction

Grades: 4–6

In the early days of America, a young man journeyed from Japan to America to settle in San Francisco and raise his family, but he found that a yearning for Japan eventually drew them all back to Japan. After his grown daughter gave birth to Allen Say, the author, Say, like his grandfather, came to visit America. Say's emotions are divided between two countries as he says, "[T]he moment I am in one country, I am homesick for the other."

Discussion and Beyond: Being a Culture Historian

With students, discuss being a culture historian as one of the world's most important jobs, and mention, "The job can be yours if you want to start now." Challenge interested students to find out through research how much they already know about a particular culture. For students who are interested in Japanese heritage, *Grandfather's Journey* provides background information to discuss the following questions:

1. What are the topics of reflection related to the family home when one leaves Japan? When one arrives in America?

2. What words describe the homes that a Japanese immigrant sees in America?

3. How do the family homes in the two countries differ?

4. What industrial advances useful in homes are available in both countries?

Target Activity: Interviewing an Immigrant

Many immigrants, like Allen Say's ancestors, came to America to seek a better life for their family. Have students interview an immigrant they know who came to this country seeking a better life for their family (if students do not know such an immigrant, help them contact one). Specifically, ask students to address three issues with their interviewee:

1. Why did you think America would be a better place to raise a family?

2. Are you glad that you raised (or are raising) your family in America? Why?

3. How would family life have been different in your former country?

Uchida, Yoshiko (1981). *A Jar of Dreams*. New York: Macmillan.

Heritage: Japanese American

Family Context:

◆ family heritage

◆ aunt-niece relationship/extended family relationships

◆ family adversity

◆ family support

Genre: historical fiction

Grades: 4–5

This is the story of an eleven-year-old Japanese American girl, Rinka, growing up in Berkeley during the Great Depression. Her Aunt Waka visits from Japan one summer and helps her and her family realize that they have strengths that can help them pursue their dreams, despite the prejudice they face. This is an accurate depiction of the struggle an extended immigrant family faces—a desire to preserve the culture of their homeland versus a desire to be accepted by mainstream American society.

Discussion and Beyond:
Pursuing a Dream

Discuss the following questions:

1. Do you know a Japanese American family who has lived in your area since the Great Depression?

2. What changed when Aunt Waka visited Rinka's family?

3. If you had been with Rinka and her family during this time, what would you have done to help them pursue their dreams? To face the prejudice of others?

4. What would you have done to help Rinka preserve her homeland culture and still be accepted by American society?

Target Activity: Family Crest

Aunt Waka helped Rinka's family concentrate on their strengths. Ask students to take a few moments to think about what makes their family (family arrangement) strong. Help them get started by offering examples of strengths—traits such as humor, talking to one another, and sharing common interests. Using tagboard and marking pens, have students make a family crest with their family name (or names, in some cases) and small pictures symbolizing their family's strengths.

Yep, Laurence (1975). *Dragonwings*. Illustrated by David Wiesner. New York: Harper & Row.

Heritage: Chinese

Family Context:

◆ family heritage

◆ father-son relationship

Genre: historical fiction

Grades: 6+

In 1903 in San Francisco, eight-year-old Moon Shadow is determined to help his father build a flying machine. Motivated by the work of Orville and Wilbur Wright, they build an airplane, called *Dragonwings*, and glide off the hills at San Francisco Bay. Moon Shadow modifies his views of the cultural stereotypes of the white people and learns that his ideas are not always accurate. He meets an Anglo-Saxon woman who is friendly and considerate, and he gains respect for her. His father expresses the differences between the two cultures with, "We see the same thing and yet find different truths."

Discussion and Beyond:
Finding Different Truths from
Our Family Experiences

On the chalkboard, write the words of Moon Shadow's father: "We see the same thing and yet find different truths." Ask for ideas as to what the father meant by this remark. Discuss how this remark is true not only of people from different cultures, but of people from diverse families as well.

Target Activity: Children in Families of All Cultures Have Dreams of Success

Select another book depicting strong characters from a different culture who strive to succeed, such as Aliki Brandenburg's (for grades 4–6) *A Weed Is a Flower* (New York: Simon & Schuster, 1968) that tells of George Washington Carver's boyhood of slavery and poverty, and his adulthood as a successful scientist. Divide the students into pairs to "read the book in one hour." To read the book in this short period of time, have each student pair select a different chapter (or chapters) to read and then summarize in writing. Students may illustrate their chapter summaries if desired. Following the chapter order of the book, have student pairs share their summaries orally with the class. After the oral summary of the book, engage the students in a discussion of the idea that girls, boys, women, and men in all cultures have dreams of success. Write the dreams of success from the selected book on the chalkboard.

Yep, Laurence (1979). *Sea Glass*. New York: Harper & Row.

Heritage: Chinese

Family Context:

+ family heritage
+ family conflict
+ father-son relationship

Genre: historical fiction

Grades: 6+

Craig copes with the unhappy experience of leaving Chinatown in San Francisco and learning to live in a non-Chinese community in a small town in California. In this transition, Craig must face all the difficulties of being a newcomer. Craig tries to make his father understand his ambitions, creating family conflict about different goals.

Discussion and Beyond: Accepting a Newcomer in Your Community

Brainstorm ways that students can accept a newcomer as a friend, a favorite classmate, and as a member of the community. Write their ideas on the chalkboard. Ask them to team up with partners and play the roles of a newcomer and a resident who implements some of the ideas on the list. Have students change roles and repeat the role play.

Target Activity: A Parent's Ambition

Have students ask their father, mother, or an adult family member about their ambitions when they were a child and if they have realized any of their goals. In class, ask students to write a paragraph describing their personal ambitions, mentioning how their goals are similar or dissimilar to their parent's goals. How do they account for the differences in ambitions, if any? Did this assignment help them understand Craig's conflict with his father? What advice would they offer Craig?

Yep, Laurence (1977). *Child of the Owl.* **New York: Harper & Row.**

Heritage: Chinese

Family Context:

✦ family heritage

✦ extended family

✦ family support

Genre: contemporary realistic fiction

Grades: 6+

Casey, a Chinese American girl, lives in San Francisco with her gambling father, Barney. When Barney is hospitalized after being beaten and robbed of his one big win, he sends Casey to live with her Uncle Phil and his family in suburbia. Casey does not get along with Uncle Phil's family, and they are horrified by her strange habits and manners, so she is sent to Chinatown to live with her grandmother, Paw Paw. At first, Casey does not like the narrow streets and alleys, or the Chinese school, but then Paw Paw tells her about Jeanie (Casey's mother) whom she never knew; about her true Chinese name; and the story of the family's owl charm. Gradually, she comes to accept herself and her heritage, and to realize that Chinatown is her home, just as it is home to Paw Paw, and it once was to her father and her mother.

Discussion and Beyond: Adjusting to a New Home

Ask students if they have ever had the experience of moving to a different country, state, city, or area within a city. What were their initial reactions to the unfamiliar place? Who in the family was most helpful in helping them make the adjustment? Why is it that people often love most that which they know best?

Target Activity: Knowing My Heritage Brings Pride

Divide the class into small groups, and have each member of the group read part of a selected book (one chapter or a certain number of pages) about their heritage. Have each student discuss within their group what they learned related to the theme "knowing one's heritage brings pride." As a class, ask the groups to contribute what they learned, and then invite students to discuss similarities among the stories that were read. Have students reassemble into groups and share examples of how knowing one's heritage brings pride.

Lord, Bette Bao (1984). *In the Year of the Boar and Jackie Robinson.* **New York: Harper & Row.**

Heritage: Chinese

Family Context:

✦ family heritage

Genre: realistic fiction

Grades: 4–6

In 1947, a Chinese child moves to Brooklyn, where she make friends of diverse backgrounds and cultures when she discovers baseball and the Brooklyn Dodgers. This is an excellent account of an immigrant girl who is a newcomer and experiences the difficulties in assimilating a different culture.

Discussion and Beyond: Empathizing with an Immigrant

Ask students to brainstorm the major difficulties facing a child coming to a different country (e.g., language is different, foods seem strange, customs are unfamiliar, etc.). Ask the students to help you list all the emotions that a child in this situation might feel (e.g., fear, anxiety, lack of confidence, sadness, etc.).

Target Activity: A Newcomer in Your Town

With students, discuss the idea of welcoming a newcomer who has come from China and settled in your town or city—she is the only Chinese student in the class, and one of only a few Asian Americans in the school. Ask the students, "What would you do?"

Suggest other situations, and have students role play brief scenes. Have students change roles and enact several versions of each situation (with different interpretations of the roles). For example:

1. You become friendly with the newcomer from China. You are together often, talk together in a friendly manner, and do things together. Your other friends make fun of you or stay away from you because of this friendship. What do you do?

2. You are hearing much talk about having a school just for newcomers because most of them are not able to speak English fluently. Play the roles of a newcomer, a teacher, a student, a principal, a parent, and the superintendent of the school district.

Golub, Matthew (1994). *The Moon Was at a Fiesta.* **Illustrated by Leovigido Martinez. New York: Tambourine.**

Heritage: Hispanic

Family Context:

✦ family heritage

Genre: folk literature

Grades: 4–5

Set in Mexico, this tale about nature explains why the moon is sometimes seen in the morning sky, as well as how the moon affects the families in Oaxaca. It seems that the moon became jealous when she heard about the celebrations, feasts, and parties that happened during the daylight hours. To change this, the moon decided to have a fiesta at night—with decorations and wooden masks—and the families agreed to stay out until the dawn to celebrate. When dawn came, however, the families were so tired that they could not go into the fields to work, and the moon became remorseful over her actions. Occasionally, though, the moon still wanted to have a fiesta, and sometimes she could be seen in the early morning sky. This is why, to this day, the families in Oaxaca can sometimes see the moon when they are up at sunrise. When they see the moon in the early morning sky, they say, "The moon was at a fiesta."

Discussion and Beyond: Questions Children Ask

Encourage children to share some questions they can recall asking their parents or caregivers about the cause of natural phenomena, such as, "What causes thunder?" or "Where does the sun go at night?" List these questions on the chalkboard. Then discuss with children why they think parents in all cultures might often fabricate responses to these questions rather than providing scientific explanations.

Target Activity: My Family's "Why Tales"

Invite the students to participate in either of the following activities:

1. Have students interview their parents, grandparents, or older relatives about stories they have heard that explain why some natural element came to be. Have students record the interview on audiocassette and play it for the class.

2. Have students write a fictional "why tale," featuring their family, about how they experienced a natural event, such as a tornado, earthquake, or flood. The tale should provide a whimsical explanation for the natural event.

Krumgold, Joseph (1953). *And Now Miguel.* Illustrated by J. Charlot. Crowell.

Heritage: Hispanic

Family Context:

◆ family heritage

◆ family problem solving

◆ family support

Genre: historical fiction

Grades: 6–8

For generations, the bilingual family of Miguel Chavez has raised sheep in New Mexico. The year that Miguel turns twelve, he longs to go with the other members of his family to take the sheep to the high pasture in the Sangre de Cristo Mountains near their home. His father tells him that he cannot go, but later Miguel is told that this year he will accompany his family. His brother, Gabriel, is being drafted into the army, and Miguel is to go in his place.

Discussion and Beyond: Joining a Family Tradition

Miguel tries earnestly to prove himself worthy to his family so he will be allowed to go with the older family members to take the sheep to the high pasture. Miguel shows others how helpful he is with the family's flock: He finds the ewes and lambs that stray from the others, and he carefully paints identical numbers on each ewe and newly born lamb at lambing time. Have students meet with partners and discuss a time when they tried to prove themselves worthy to a family member so that they could join a family tradition reserved for older family members (or discuss someone they know who tried to prove themselves worthy). Were they successful? Did their success or failure change their role in family life?

Target Activity:
A Wish That Affects the Family

When Miguel asks his father if he can go to the high pasture with the others, he is told "No"—but Miguel does not give up. He prays to the patron saint of the village that his wish be granted, however the saint can arrange it. When his beloved nineteen-year-old brother, Gabriel, is drafted into the army, Miguel is asked to go to the high pasture in his place. When his brother is drafted, Miguel regrets his wish and prays to the patron saint to take back his wish.

Recount these events for students, and ask them to reflect upon a time when they wished for something but later, when it was granted, regretted the wish. Have students write a confidential journal entry about their reflections and what they would do differently if they could change the past (if students have not had this experience, have them write about an imagined wish). Have students include in their writing the effects the wish had on family members.

Castaneda, Omar S. (1991). *Among the Volcanoes.* **New York: Dutton.**

Heritage: Guatemalan/Mayan

Family Context:

+ **family heritage**
+ **family adversity**
+ **family illness**
+ **family problem solving**
+ **family support**

Genre: contemporary realistic fiction

Grades: 6–8

When her mother becomes ill, Isabel Pacay, a Mayan girl living in contemporary Guatamala, cares for her and the household, but she continues to pursue her dreams—she wants a chance to go to school—and to search for her identity in a world filled with upheaval. The meeting of the old ways and the new ways is depicted in the story when her father makes the sacrifice of a bird to the old gods but also offers a prayer to the Christian god. Isabel faces a dilemma between the old ways and the new ways: Should she stay and marry her boyfriend Lucas Choy (the old way)? Or should she leave and go to school (the new way)? Should she rely upon the sanjorin, the local village healer, to help her mother (the old way)? Or should she rely upon Western medicine (the new way)?

Discussion and Beyond: Focusing on Likenesses and Differences

Ask the students to reflect upon likenesses and differences among themselves and Isabel and her family. Discuss the likenesses and differences, and record them on the chalkboard. Divide students into partnerships, and have one student begin a dialogue with: "I am like Isabel Pacay because . . ." Have the other student conclude the dialogue with: "I am different from Isabel Pacay because . . ." Have students switch roles with their partners, and then have students change partners and repeat the activity.

Target Activity:
A Dialogue with Parents

Ask students to think of a time when they wanted something, or wanted to do something, but their parents or guardian disagreed with their request. Would such disagreements happen more often for people like Isabel, who was adjusting to a culture different from her parents' culture? Have students write a dialogue between themselves and their parents or guardian that, as best as they can recall, captures the logical arguments put forth by both sides. After completing the dialogue, ask students if this activity in any way helped them better understand the point of view of their parents or guardian.

Acierno, Maria Armengol (1994). *Children of Flight Pedro Pan.* **New York: Silver Moon Press.**

Heritage: Cuban

Family Context:

◆ **family heritage**

◆ **extended family**

◆ **sibling relationship**

Genre: historical fiction

Grades: 4–6

In the 1960s, ten-year-old Maria and her eight-year-old brother, José, are sent by their well-to-do parents by airplane (*Flight Pedro Pan*) from Cuba to America because of political turmoil. Arrangements are made for them to live with a distant relative and her mother. The children try to do well in school, help with the chores, and cope with the problems an immigrant faces—coping with a new country, culture, and language. Finally, their mother and father arrive, bringing news that their sugarcane plantation has been lost. Nevertheless, the family's reunion is a joyful one after the long separation. Informative notes about Cuban politics of the time are included at the end of the book.

Discussion and Beyond:
Identifying with Maria and José

Elicit students' thoughts about the experiences of immigrant children in America:

1. when learning a new language,

2. when interacting with a new culture, and

3. when living in a new country.

Discuss with students how they identify with Maria and José.

Target Activity: Coping with a New Country, Culture, and Language

Have students work with partners to list positive (pluses) and negative (minuses) aspects of immigrating to and coping with a new country, culture, and language. Have partnerships pair together and combine their lists, adding and deleting aspects as desired. Have each group share their list as well as their reasons for including (or excluding) each aspect.

Bouchard, Lois (1969). *The Boy Who Wouldn't Talk.* **New York: Doubleday.**

Heritage: Puerto Rican

Family Context:

✦ family heritage

✦ family adversity

✦ family problem solving

✦ family support

Genre: contemporary realistic fiction

Grades: 4–8

In New York City, Carlos and his family are newcomers from Puerto Rico. Carlos is frustrated with his language problem, so he decides to stop talking—in English and in Spanish. When he meets Ricky Hernandez, a blind boy who asks for directions to get home, he notices that Ricky cannot see street signs he needs to find his way through the neighborhood. Carlos helps Ricky by reading aloud the signs for him.

Discussion and Beyond:
Learning a New Language

Ask students to share summaries of stories they have read that have the theme that language problems can be overcome when moving to a new country or an area where a different language is dominant. Discuss the difficulties of living in a world with myriad languages and how these barriers can be overcome.

Target Activity:
Helping Newcomers

In small groups, have students devise strategies they might use to help children coming to their school from other countries, especially those for whom English is a second language. Invite students to create and perform skits that show others how to effectively welcome newcomers using the strategies they have devised.

Yolen, Jane (1988). *The Devil's Arithmetic.* **New York: Viking/Kestrel.**

Heritage: European

Family Context:

✦ family heritage

✦ family concerns

✦ family conflict

Genre: historical fiction

Grades: 7–8

In this story of transformation, Hannah, weary of hearing her Jewish relatives tell of the Holocaust, wishes to be somewhere else. Her wish is granted when she steps out of her family's apartment and into a small village in Nazi-occupied Poland—she has become the villager Chaya, whose name means "Life." Chaya experiences the Holocaust. She is put on a cattle car with her family and friends and then branded, stripped, and shaved when she arrived at the concentration camp. When Hannah again finds herself at her family's apartment, she appreciates her relatives for who they are and what they know.

Discussion and Beyond: Appreciating Family Members

Divide the class into small groups, and ask students to think of their family members, what they do, and what they know. Have groups discuss the contributions their family members make to the community. Have groups discuss how they show their appreciation of their family members for who they are and what they know.

Target Activity: A Look at Family Heritage

Have students interview older family members about experiences they have had that differ significantly from life today. Ask students to write an essay reflecting on the experiences that were shared, concluding with new appreciations of who the relatives are and what they know.

MIXED-RACE FAMILIES

Ferris, Jeri (1991). *Native American Doctor: The Story of Susan LaFlesche Picotte.* **New York: Carolrhoda.**

Heritage: Native American

Family Context:

◆ mixed-race family

◆ family heritage

◆ two-parent family

Genre: biography

Grades: 5–7

Susan LaFlesche was raised among the Native Americans of Omaha. Susan's mother was Native American. Her father was half French and half Native American and he believed in learning the ways of the white people. Susan attended mission school and college, and became the first Native American female physician. She returned to the Omaha reservation in Nebraska to serve as a government doctor until ill health forced her to retire. However, she continued to pursue her interests in health-related issues and Native American concerns. The author has compiled this biography using primary sources, such as her letters, family papers, and photographs from government archives. Interviews with her descendants are included.

Discussion and Beyond: Appreciating Two Cultures

Ask students to consider the advantages and the disadvantages of growing up in two cultures. Encourage students to reread parts of the book to find specific ways that Susan's father and others around her helped her appreciate both of her cultural heritages. Ask students, "How did Susan come to be proud of herself and very successful despite sometimes feeling torn between two worlds?"

Target Activity: A History of Family Life

Have students reread parts of the book and take notes in a "family biography journal" (spiral-bound notebook) about the family life of LaFlesche (or have students study another historical figure). Tell the students that they are ready to assemble a history of LaFlesche's family life:

1. Have students brainstorm, from memory, the events in LaFlesche's family life. Write the events on the chalkboard. Encourage the students to be selective and include the most dramatic events and the events LaFlesche felt most proud of achieving and those that made her parents proud.

2. Engage the students as a class in pantomiming motions that depict the action of the listed events.

3. Ask the students to open their biography journals and look through their notes for more events to add to the list on the chalkboard. Pantomime these actions as a class.

Fritz, Jean (1982). *The Double Life of Pocahontas*. Illustrated by Ed Young. New York: Putnam Group.

Heritage: Native American

Family Context:

✦ mixed-race family

✦ family heritage

✦ two-parent family

Genre: biography

Grades: 4–6

This biography details the life story of this Native American princess and her role in helping the English settlers survive in the unfamiliar conditions at Jamestown. After developing a friendship with John Smith, Pocahontas married John Rolfe. When she later travels to England with Rolfe, she fulfills her double life—as a Native American princess and as the wife of an Englishman.

Discussion and Beyond: Pocahontas: Native American Princess and English Wife*

*Note: This activity is to begin prior to reading the book and continue while reading the book, one chapter at a time.

With students, discuss the title of this book, *The Double Life of Pocahontas*, and elicit what these words mean to them. Ask students to fold a sheet of paper in half lengthwise to make two columns, and have them label the left-hand column "I Expect to Hear About. . . ." Each day before reading a chapter to the class, ask the students to sketch or write in the left-hand column something

they expect to hear about Pocahontas and her double life. Have students listen as you read aloud a chapter of the biography. In the right-hand column, have them summarize the chapter that was just heard or read. Discuss the chapter, and ask the students to share with the class what they predicted or wrote if, indeed, they heard about this event in the princess's life.

Target Activity: Two Dwellings

Divide the class into small groups. Engage half the groups in a collaborative project of constructing a small-scale Native American dwelling, and the other half of the groups, an English home of the times—two types of dwellings that represent the double life that Pocahontas lived. Display the dwellings, and engage the students in imagining a day in the life of Pocahontas, first in her Native American dwelling, and then in her English home. Have them imagine how her life would be the same or different in the two environments and list their thoughts individually. Invite students to read their list to the class. Collate students' reflections into a class book titled *The Double Life of Pocahontas*.

Pullman, Philip (1992). *The Broken Bridge.* **New York: Knopf.**

Heritage: African American

Family Context:

◆ mixed-race family

◆ single father

Genre: contemporary realistic fiction

Grades: 6–8

Ginny is the child of a black Haitian artist and a white British father. She is faced with a number of nagging questions about her family history. Ginny's mother died, she was told, when she was a baby, and she has always been close to her father. Now, however, she is hearing rumors that her father once spent time in jail. Her father will not discuss their family history. Ginny is confronted by the disturbing news that she has a half brother, Robert, who is coming to live with them. As she struggles to accept the sullen Robert as a member of her family, she learns that it was Robert's mother, not hers, to whom her father was married. She is, in other words, illegitimate. The final blow for Ginny comes when she meets her mother, who is not dead after all, but Ginny has no interest in pursuing a relationship with her. Ginny eventually learns to accept the facts of her family life and her biracial identity.

Discussion and Beyond: What Affects a Family's Life?

Meet with interested students in small groups or individually to discuss the following social issues described by the author: child abuse, homosexuality, and interracial marriage. Discuss how these issues have affected students, just as they affected Ginny, who felt the usual confusion of all adolescents about growing up and about her family life.

Target Activity: A Family's Soap Opera

The dramatic twists and turns in Ginny's young life would make an excellent soap opera, if done respectfully and sensitively. Have small groups of students select scenes from the book to act out for the class. Afterwards, discuss with students how such reenactments helped them better appreciate the feelings of all the characters in the book.

Rosenberg, Maxine B. (1986). *Living in Two Worlds.* **Photographs by George Ancona. New York: Lothrop, Lee & Shepard.**

Heritage: African American

Family Context:

◆ mixed-race families

Genre: biography

Grades: 4–8

These stories concern the lives of biracial children. Illustrated with black-and-white photographs by George Ancona, the stories are told by the children themselves. Parents, grandparents, friends, and classmates are, in general, friendly and understanding, but some are tactless and hurtful.

There is some discussion about feeling "different," which many such children experience, but their responses show remarkable maturity (e.g., "Is that your father or your friend?" "He's my father *and* my friend."). The family values of many cultures are demonstrated abundantly. The only drawback to the book is that in every instance, one parent in the biracial couple is white; a story about a non-white biracial family would have provided another important perspective. An afterword by a psychologist provides statistics on biracial children and a discussion of their usually successful adjustment to their heritage.

Discussion and Beyond: Adjusting to a Family's Heritage

Pair students together, and have them discuss concerns about their lives related to their families (or families they know). Have students consider how these same concerns might be magnified in the lives of biracial children. Ask them to contribute examples of times when family members were friendly and understanding to them as well as times when someone was tactless and hurtful. Discuss times when they have felt "different" for one reason or another. Ask them what they might do to help a peer when they realize that the peer has concerns about being different.

Target Activity: I Am Like and Unlike My Family Member

Even in cases where children have been adopted, they usually acquire certain traits, physical attributes, or other characteristics that are similar to those of other family members. In some cases, the children are proud of these likenesses, and in other cases, they would prefer not to resemble family members. Discuss this with students, and ask them to think of one way that they are like a family member (especially in personality or temperament). Have students draw a picture of themselves and that family member, underscoring the similarity. Invite students to share and discuss their drawings in small groups.

Relationships Within Families

SIBLING RELATIONSHIPS

Metzger, Lois (1992). *Barry's Sister*. New York: Atheneum.

Heritage: European

Family Context:

◆ sibling relationship

◆ family adversity

◆ family illness

◆ new baby

Genre: contemporary realistic fiction

Grades: 5–8

The news of her mother's pregnancy is a great shock for fourteen-year-old Ellen, but she is even more upset when she learns that her new brother, Barry, has a strange disease called cerebral palsy. This is a sensitively written novel that deals with the issues that a family must face when misfortune befalls them. It is especially noteworthy that the problem is seen from the perspective of a sibling.

Discussion and Beyond:
Dealing with Misfortune

Discuss with students how Ellen's feelings about the new baby changed from before the baby was born until she realized that the baby had cerebral palsy. Discuss how this misfortune brought the family closer together. Ask students to share examples of misfortune in families they know about or have read about (or in their families, if they feel comfortable doing this). Did the misfortune bring the family closer together or drive the members apart? How did the misfortune do this?

Target Activity:
A Case Study of *Barry's Sister*

To help students understand and empathize with other young people and their family problems, discuss Ellen's problems, and her solutions to the problems, as presented in the story. Discuss alternative ways to cope with these problems. Ask the students to think of the consequences of these alternatives, identify the best solutions, and support their conclusions with specific reasons. Record the problems, alternative solutions, and consequences on the chalkboard.

Lynch, Chris (1994). *Iceman.* **San Francisco: HarperCollins.**

Heritage: European

Family Context:

✦ sibling relationship

✦ family conflict

Genre: contemporary realistic fiction

Grades: 8+

Fourteen-year-old Eric is called the iceman because he plays mean and hard during his hockey games, behavior that his father encourages. His mother is very religious and frowns upon this behavior. His older brother, Duane, is the only one who keeps Eric's spirits up and is supportive of who he is, using humor and showing him new ways to cope with his anger.

Discussion and Beyond: Family Members Can Help Each Other

With the students, discuss how Eric's brother, Duane, helped keep Eric's spirits up. Invite the students to think of ways they could help keep another family member's spirits up, just as Duane did for Eric. In what ways did Duane use humor? How could the students convince others to use humor in these ways? What new ways to cope with anger could students share with family members to improve their lives together?

Target Activity: Letters to Duane

Divide the class into pairs. Ask each student to write about a family problem they have recently experienced (the problem can be real or imagined so all students will feel comfortable with the activity), in the form of an "anonymous" letter to Duane. Have students trade letters with their partners. Ask them to consider the way Duane sensitively, and with humor, helped Eric with his problems, so that Eric felt better. Have students try to help their partner in a similar way, by being positive and upbeat about the problem. Assemble the letters into a classroom book of advice for dealing with family problems.

Strasser, Todd (1992). *The Diving Bell.* **New York: Scholastic.**

Heritage: Native American

Family Context:

✦ sibling relationship

✦ family crisis

✦ family problem solving

Genre: historical fiction

Grades: 4–6

During a heavy storm, several ships carrying gold taken by the Spanish conquistadors sink off the coast of Mexico. Culca, a young Mexican girl, Culca's brother, and other native divers are taken to recover the gold. Knowing the danger of diving in the dangerous waters and because of his age, Culca devises a plan to save her brother's life. This is not only a story about family problem solving, but it also addresses issues of this time period (the mid-1800s)—the role of the church in the family lives of the community, the Spanish conquistadors' exploitation of the native people, and the role of women and girls in Mexican life.

Discussion and Beyond:
Facing a Family Problem

Write the word *problem* on the chalkboard and ask students what this word means to them. Discuss the problems encountered in family life. Culca's problem was to think of a way to save her brother's life. Have the students, in girl-boy partnerships, discuss Culca's problem as if they were seeing it through the eyes of Culca and her brother. Ask them to discuss what they would have done in this situation and write down their plan of action. Have the partnerships discuss the possible consequences of carrying out their plan.

Martin, Rafe (1992). *The Rough-Face Girl.* **Illustrated by David Shannon. New York: Putnam Group.**

Heritage: Native American

Family Context:

◆ sibling relationship

◆ family conflict

Genre: folk literature

Grades: 4–6

In this Algonquin folktale, analagous to Cinderella, the youngest of three sisters burns her face and hair while tending the fire in her home. Her face becomes rough from the scarring. Like her sisters, she wants to marry the "Invisible Being" who lives in the large wigwam across the village. Her sisters falsely claim that they can see this being, but she is the only one who truly sees him and can answer correctly the questions asked by the being's sister. She marries the "Invisible Being" in a fairy-tale-type ending.

Discussion and Beyond:
A Cinderella-Type Family
Is Found in Many Stories

Suggest other Cinderella-type stories that depict disturbed sibling relationships. Have students read the stories and tell the class what similarities and differences they found in the family relationships. As one example, for students in grades 6–8, suggest Sherry Garland's realistic story *Song of the Buffalo Boy* (New York: Harcourt Brace Jovanovich, 1992): Loi, a modern-day Cinderella, cannot go to school in the village but is made to work for her uncle's family. Only Khai, a buffalo boy, notices her value. When Loi is promised in marriage against her wishes, she runs away with Khai and eventually finds herself alone in Ho Chi Minh City. There, she finds a "godfather" (who is really a Vietnam veteran), and he sponsors Loi's journey to the United States.

Target Activity:
Changing Sibling Character Traits

Using *The Rough-Face Girl* or another Cinderella-type story, have students study the character traits of the main characters (in this type of folk literature, the characters are almost always one-dimensional, i.e., beautiful or ugly, kind or cruel). Ask students to select their favorite story from this genre and rewrite it, reversing the major traits of the main character. For example, the Cinderella character could be portrayed as mean instead of kind, and the stepsisters could be intelligent and helpful instead of petty and interfering. Invite students to share how sibling interactions changed in their story version.

Monroe, Jean Guard, and Ray A. Williamson (1987). *They Dance in the Sky: Native American Star Myths.* **Illustrated by Edgar Stewart. Boston: Houghton Mifflin.**

Heritage: Native American

Family Context:

✦ sibling relationship

✦ family concerns

Genre: folk literature

Grades: 6–8

The first two chapters contain Native American stories about the Seven Sisters (the Pleiades) and the Big Dipper. The remaining chapters contain other Native American star myths, divided by geographic region.

Discussion and Beyond: Family Relationships Help Explain Sky-Origin Stories

With the students, discuss the family relationships that help explain some of the different sky-origin stories. Collate information about family relationships from these folk stories into a classroom chart to be used as a future reading reference.

Target Activity: Families in Sky-Origin Stories

Have students study several of the sky-origin stories in this book. Encourage students to write an original story that explains the origin of the sky, including their family members as main characters as well as characteristic family interactions and family anecdotes. Have them illustrate, bind, and laminate their stories, and place the stories near the chart of family relationships (see above) to complete a classroom display about families in sky-origin stories.

Cookson, Catherine (1975). *Our John Willie.* **New York: New American Library.**

Heritage: European

Family Context:

✦ sibling relationship

✦ family member with a physical disability

Genre: historical fiction

Grades: 5–8

This gripping historical novel set in the mine country of northern England portrays the unselfish love between two orphaned brothers (one a deaf mute). The presence of the ominous figure, Miss Peamarsh, the village's eccentric, adds a wonderfully gothic tone to the novel. Teachers, librarians, and parents may want to make a note of pages 152–53, which concern a child born out of wedlock.

This book is often shelved among adult fiction titles but may be used advisedly with older students.

Discussion and Beyond: Brotherly Love

On the chalkboard or an overhead transparency, list the ways the two brothers in this story showed their courage and commitment to each other.

Did they display what is commonly considered "brotherly love"? Ask the students who have siblings to recount specific incidents of brotherly or sisterly love that has been displayed toward them, or that they have displayed toward a sibling.

Target Activity: Sibling Awards

Have students think about their siblings, or the siblings of friends, and choose one who displays the characteristics of brotherly or sisterly love like the brothers in *Our John Willie*. Ask the class to design a sibling award with an appropriate symbol or logo. Have each child make an award for their chosen sibling and explain to the rest of the class why the person whom they chose is deserving of the honor. Encourage students to present the award to their sibling.

Wright, Betty Ren (1991). *The Scariest Night.* **New York: Holiday House.**

Heritage: European

Family Context:

◆ sibling relationship

◆ adopted child/adoptive family

◆ family conflicts

Genre: contemporary realistic fiction

Grades: 5–7

During a summer in a run-down apartment building in Milwaukee, Erin Lindsay enjoys an "only child" status until her parents adopt nine-year-old Cowper, who is a musical genius. Her parents, obsessed with their genius son, want Cowper to attend a nearby conservatory and study music. They do not realize that Erin's new relationship with Molly Panca, an elderly medium, is about to change their lives during an impending, frightening night.

Discussion and Beyond: Getting Along with an Adopted Sibling

Ask students if they have ever known a friend who felt jealous of or resented an adopted sibling. Explain that this feeling is perfectly normal. Ask students to talk with partners about a time when they or a friend felt jealous of an adopted sibling. Ask the students to write a paragraph about a time when an adopted sibling did something that upset them or a friend.

Target Activity: Problems with Family Members

Encourage students to participate in one of the following activities:

1. Have students write a dialogue that they or a friend could have with a friend or relative about a problem with a sibling or family member.

2. Have students write a paragraph about a problem with an adopted or biological sibling. Have them close the paragraph by revealing how they felt after sharing their problem with the sibling and the family.

Cooney, Caroline (1991). *Twenty Pageants Later.* New York: Bantam.

Heritage: European

Family Context:

◆ sibling relationship

◆ family conflict

Genre: contemporary realistic fiction

Grades: 6–8

This story contrasts the attention and acclaim given to sixteen-year-old Dane McKane, a "professional beauty contestant," with the meager recognition given to her eighth-grade sister, Scottie-Anne, who is the youngest student in the state to be accepted into Yale's Russian Language Program. The story is told through the eyes of young Scottie-Anne and is an evenhanded examination of sibling rivalry, beauty pageants, and the family tension between the superficial and the substantive.

Discussion and Beyond: Major and Minor Problems in a Family

With the students, discuss Scottie-Anne's feelings as she struggled to find her place in the family. Have students mention the superficial and substantive things that cause family stress. List their ideas on the chalkboard.

Target Activity: Handling Sibling Rivalry

Ask students if they have ever felt resentment toward a sibling or relative, just as Scottie-Anne felt toward her sister when the family made more of a fuss over Dane's beauty than Scottie-Anne's good grades. Encourage them to confront the sibling or relative whom they resent in a letter that explains their feelings. Explain that the letter need not be actually given to the sibling or relative; it is only a way for them to sort out feelings that may not be the fault of the sibling or relative. To help students clarify their feelings, provide a template such as the one provided below.

Dear _____ ,
       (name of sibling or relative)

    You may be _____ , but I am
         (your sibling's or relative's strengths, talents, and good qualities)

_____ . Please recognize the things that I can do.
(your strengths, talents, and good qualities)

I can _____ , and I feel _____ . I love you

just the way you are. I hope you love me just the way I am.

Love,

_____

Anderson, Margaret (1980). *The Journey of the Shadow Baires*. New York: Knopf.

Heritage: Scottish

Family Context:

✦ sibling relationships

Genre: historical fiction

Grades: 6–7

After her father's death in Glasgow, Elspeth carries out his plans to homestead in Canada. Elspeth and her brother Robbie (with his toy, Pig-Bear) stow away on board a ship. To avoid the authorities, she creates the game of "shadow children" (Shadow Baires) to encourage her brother to be quiet and to keep out of sight. After a long ocean voyage and a train trip across Canada, Elspeth becomes ill in Saskatchewan and, later, Robbie disappears. It takes weeks to find him and to find a new home.

Discussion and Beyond:
Taking Care of a Younger Sibling

To avoid the authorities, Elspeth created the game of shadow children (Shadow Baires) on board the ship to encourage her brother to be quiet and to keep out of sight. Invite the students to share their experiences of caring for a younger brother or sister, whom they protected from harm in some way.

Target Activity:
Creating a Game for a Sibling

In small groups, have students collaborate to create a new game that they can teach a younger brother or sister, just as Elspeth did. Have each group test their newly created game on others in the class. Encourage students who have younger siblings to teach them the game at home. Have students share with the class the reactions of younger brothers and sisters to the game and to the attention given them by their older sibling.

Vogel, Ilse-Margaret (1976). *My Twin Sister Erika*. New York: Harper & Row.

Heritage: German

Family Context:

✦ sibling relationship

✦ death in the family

✦ family concerns

Genre: contemporary realistic fiction

Grades: 4–6

This book, one of a series about a young German girl, Inge, and her twin sister, Erika, is a must—not only for twins but for all young girls who must fight for their identities. Told from Inge's point of view, the story powerfully portrays the sisters' struggle with friends and family, who constantly compare them or confuse them with each other. Inge reveals her feelings about identical clothing, cherished items, and deep secrets. Just when the sisters seem to be developing separate identities, Erika dies. The death is handled in a sensitive, poignant way that allows the reader to vicariously experience Inge's feelings of loss and her courage in confronting her pain. Inge begins to discover a new place for herself and a new importance in her mother's life. Her newfound bond with her mother helps Inge overcome her grief.

Discussion and Beyond: Sibling Comparisons

Poll the students with a show of hands as to how many have older brothers or sisters. Record the information (brothers, sisters, number) on a data chart on the chalkboard. Ask these students to share if they were ever compared positively or negatively with these older siblings. How did it make them feel?

Target Activity: Who Am I?

Ask students to divide a piece of paper into two columns. At the top of one column, have them write "I am. . . ." At the top of the other column, have them write "My sister/brother is. . . ." Encourage students to think of as many similarities and differences as they can between themselves and their siblings. Urge them to confine their list to personality traits and qualities rather than physical features. For those students who have no older siblings, have them choose a younger sibling, cousin, or friend of the family with whom they have been compared. Have students discuss whether they think that the fight for identity between twins or siblings would be markedly different in other cultures. Why?

Beatty, Patricia (1978). *Wait for Me, Watch for Me, Eula Bee.* **New York: Morrow.**

Heritage: European

Family Context:

✦ sibling relationships

✦ family crisis

✦ family problem solving

Genre: historical fiction

Grades: 6+

In this spellbinding, realistic portrayal of Lewallen, a Texas teenager's painful struggle to free his four-year-old sister from her Comanche captors, the reader finds a violent, yet often tender, portrayal of Western family life in the 1860s. With historical precision, the author presents the Indian wars from Native American and white perspectives. The book abounds with fascinating facts about Native American and frontier life.

Discussion and Beyond: What Is Special About Siblings?

Ask students who have siblings to share special activities they share with their brothers or sisters. Ask students to share what things their siblings do

that irritate them. In what ways are sibling relationships the same as other friendships? In what ways are they different? Discuss how sibling relationships in other cultures, specifically Native American culture, compare to students' sibling relationships. Are there are any "truths" regarding sibling relationships that span all cultures?

Target Activity: What Would You Do for a Family Member?

Discuss Lewallen's courageous attempt to rescue his younger sister. Ask students if they have ever saved a family member from disaster (or if they have ever been saved by a family member). Have them write an essay about this event. For students who have not experienced such heroics, invite them to write a fictional account of their successful attempt to save a family member from a natural disaster. Encourage students to use realistic dialogue that will allow readers to vicariously experience the event.

Jaffe, Nina (1995). *Older Brother, Younger Brother: A Korean Folktale.* **Illustrated by Louise August. New York: Penguin.**

Heritage: Asian/Korean

Family Context:

✦ sibling relationship

Genre: folktale

Grades: 4–6

The satisfying triumph of the underdog is the motif in this classic folktale. After Hungbu's greedy older brother, Nolbu, forces the family to leave their home, Hungbu must work hard to provide for his family. He is rewarded one day for his act of kindness to a sparrow. Nolbu learns that hard work and kindness bring rewards of the heart. The muted watercolor illustrations evoke the cultural context of this ancient tale, and an author's note adds interesting background information.

Discussion and Beyond: Is Kindness Always Rewarded?

Discuss how folktales represent life in simplistic ways: Characters are either good or bad, and good deeds and bad deeds are rewarded and punished, respectively. Ask students the following questions:

1. In real life, are good deeds always rewarded? Are bad deeds always punished?

2. Why, then, do people often choose to do the right thing?

3. How are people taught right from wrong?

4. How could this story be revised to make it more realistic?

Target Activity: Intangible Rewards

Ask students if they have ever done things that were not expected of them to help members of their family. How did family members respond? On the chalkboard or an overhead transparency, brainstorm with students a list of intangible rewards that family members use to show appreciation. Pair students together to discuss the value of intangible rewards as opposed to monetary rewards or other tangible ways of showing appreciation.

ABSENT PARENT

Orlev, Uri (1984). *The Island on Bird Street.* **Boston: Houghton Mifflin.**

Heritage: Polish

Family Context:

✦ absent father

✦ family crisis

✦ father-son relationship

Genre: historical fiction

Grades: 4+

This story portrays how Alex, a young boy, and others survive in the Jewish ghetto of Warsaw, Poland. During World War II, Alex converts a bombed-out building into a shelter, similar to the desert island refuge in *Robinson Crusoe*, one of his favorite books. Like Crusoe, Alex is fearful and lonely, but learns to survive during the Holocaust. Alex sees the capture of his Jewish family and friends, and he cares for a wounded resistance fighter. In the end, Alex's father returns: He finds Alex in the bombed-out building, where he promised to wait, and takes him into the forest to be with partisans who are resisting the Nazis.

Discussion and Beyond: Promising to Wait for a Family Member

With the students, discuss what it means to make a promise to a family member. Write students' interpretations on the chalkboard. Throughout the story, the author focuses on Alex's survival as a "family of one" as he waits, keeping his promise. If appropriate, have the students discuss their experience of keeping a similar promise.

Target Activity: Surviving in a War

Have students play the role of Alex and write an entry on a simulated diary page describing what he did to survive during a particular day and how he feels about his promise to his father. Engage students in writing a second diary entry describing the night Alex is reunited with his father and taken into the forest to be with the partisans. Encourage the students to share their entries in small groups.

Mayer, Harry (1986). *Cave Under the City.* **New York: Crowell.**

Heritage: European

Family Context:

✦ absent father

✦ sibling relationship

✦ family adversity

✦ family illness

Genre: historical fiction

Grades: 4–6

In New York during the Great Depression, Tolley Holtz and his friends like to hang around together and talk. Because Tolley's father has no job and his mother has to work, Tolley often ends up caring for his little brother, Bubber. At times, Tolley adores his brother and worries about him. At other times, his little brother annoys him, and Tolley is lectured about being older and helping out the family when times are so hard. Tolley's father leaves the family to find work in another city. One day, Tolley and his brother come home from school and find that their mother is ill and has been taken to the hospital. Tolley becomes frightened when he realizes that, suddenly, he is in charge of the family.

Discussion and Beyond: Helping Out in a Family

Ask students to help you list the chores Tolley was called upon to perform in his family. Have each student compare these family responsibilities with their chores. Why did Tolley have so much responsibility for his younger sibling? How did it help and hinder him? Ask students to share how family responsibilities are delegated in their families. Who determines what should be done by whom? Do family responsibilities change when there is a family problem or crisis, such as illness?

Target Activity: If I Were in Charge of the Family . . .

Divide the class into partnerships, and have them discuss what they would do if they were in charge of their family during an emergency, just as Tolley did. How would they get food to eat? How would they find shelter? What work would they try to do? Have one student record the group's ideas and then share them with the class.

Hotze, Sollace (1991). *Summer Endings.* **New York: Clarion.**

Heritage: European

Family Context:
+ absent father
+ sibling relationships

Genre: historical fiction

Grades: 5-7

In May 1945 in Chicago, at the end of the World War II, twelve-year-old Christine Kosinksi and her older sister, Rosie, wait for news of their father, who was captured in Poland when the Germans invaded. They live in a multiethnic neighborhood where everyone knows the business of everyone else. At the end of the summer, on Rosie's wedding day, the girls receive news of their father. The story recounts nostalgic times—Wrigley Field; ice cream sodas at a local malt shop; and the fairyland beauty of the Aragon Ballroom, where Christine goes to her first dance.

Discussion and Beyond: A Fatherless Family During World War II

Role play a discussion between Christine and Rosie about whether it is right to fight with guns if you think the situation demands it. Ask the students to follow up with a brief discussion about the extent to which Americans were right to fight against Germany and how the war affected American families.

Target Activity: War and the Family

Engage the students in collecting information about Germany's invasion of Poland. Ask students to imagine that they and their immediate family members were alive during this time. Have students create a diary documenting their feelings and the feelings of family members about the events related to the war.

Loredo, Betsy (1995). *Faraway Families.* **New York: Silver Moon.**

Heritage: All

Family Context:

✦ absent family members

Genre: nonfiction

Grades: 4–8

The author offers useful ideas to help family members feel closer to those family members who are absent, for any reason. She suggests creating family trees and sending photos, handmade pictures of family members and family activities, letters, videotapes, and customized "care packages." Chapters, diagrams, and black-and-white illustrations organize the textual information, and a helpful glossary defines unfamiliar terms.

Discussion and Beyond: Communicating Long-Distance*

*Note: This activity precedes the reading of the book.

Discuss with students the difficulties involved in any long-distance relationship. Explain that a relationship can still thrive long-distance if both sides care enough to make the effort. Before reading *Faraway Families*, ask students to brainstorm ways to continue a loving relationship with an absent family member. Write the ideas on the chalkboard and augment them after reading the book.

Target Activity: Feeling Closer to Absent Loved Ones

From the ideas suggested in the book as well as the ideas brainstormed by students prior to reading (see "Discussion and Beyond"), ask students to create and send a loving communication to a faraway loved one. When the communications have been received, invite students to share how their communication might help the relationship.

Temple, Frances (1993). *Grab Hands and Run.* **New York: Orchard.**

Heritage: Salvadoran

Family Context:

✦ absent father

✦ family crisis

✦ family support

Genre: contemporary realistic fiction

Grades: 6–8

Twelve-year-old Felipe; his young sister, Romy; and their mother, Paloma must leave El Salvador when Felipe's father, a political activist, disappears. Felipe's family members "grab hands and run," journeying to Canada. The arduous trip is filled with bribes, lies, and luck as they cross from one country into another, always fearing for their lives.

Discussion and Beyond: Wondering If You Will Be Met

In the story, Felipe's family members were always wondering if their father would meet them when they reached their destination in Canada. Ask students to think of a time when they were supposed to meet a family member somewhere, and the person was delayed, causing the student anxiety. Invite students to share the experience with a neighbor student in the classroom. As a class, discuss the importance of family members having love and respect for one another and how this love and respect can help one cope with a difficult situation, such as waiting expectantly for someone who is delayed. Discuss other family situations in which love and respect can help a family member cope with a difficult experience.

Target Activity: Careers and Their Effect on Families

Discuss with students how Felipe's father's career, and his resulting absence, affected the rest of the family. Ask students to write a paragraph explaining how the jobs or careers of their parents effect their family life. Have students include the advantages and disadvantages of their parents' professions.

Emmerich, Elsbeth (1992). *My Childhood in Nazi Germany.* **New York: Watts.**

Heritage: European

Family Context:

+ **absent father**
+ **family crisis**
+ **family concerns**
+ **intergenerational relationship**

Genre: historical fiction

Grades: 5–8

This is a memoir of a non-Jewish, middle-class German family during World War II. Five-year-old Elsbeth knew that the war took her father away, that her grandfather was periodically arrested for his socialist activities, and that her mother lost her coaching job because she refused to join the Nazi party. This compelling story describes, in poignant detail, Elsbeth's sometimes ambivalent feelings about her family members' brave, but dangerous actions.

Discussion and Beyond: War and Its Effect on Family Life

With the students, discuss the hardships Elsbeth's family experienced during the war. Ask students if they have heard their parents or other relatives talk about what family life was like during a war. Pair students together to discuss the stories they have heard and to compare these stories with the events of Elsbeth's life.

Target Activity: Family Life During World War II

Invite a friend or a member of the community who grew up in the United States or Europe during World War II to visit the class for an interview. Before the interview, ask students to make a list of questions about family life during the war. Screen the questions for duplications and appropriateness. The following questions should be included:

1. What was family life like?
2. How did the war affect members of the family?
3. How did life change for the family when the war ended?

After the interview, discuss with students how family life during World War II was different from and similar to family life today.

Stowe, Cynthia (1992). *Dear Mom, in Ohio for a Year.* **New York: Scholastic.**

Heritage: European

Family Context:

+ absent mother
+ aunt-niece relationship
+ uncle-niece relationship
+ family conflict
+ extended family

Genre: contemporary realistic fiction

Grades: 4–7

Cassie, a sixth-grader, is left by her mother to stay with her Aunt Emily and Uncle Fred in their rural Vermont home while her mother pursues an exciting career opportunity. This change in her family situation makes Cassie feel distanced from her mother as well as her aunt and uncle. However, Mrs. Kolish, Cassie's sensitive teacher, helps Cassie regain her sense of humor and teaches her to use writing to express her feelings. She also helps Cassie to use writing as a kind of catharsis, to help cope with and analyze her problems. As she adapts to a different life, Cassie expresses her feelings with letters to her mother and finds a way to share her feelings with her aunt and uncle.

Discussion and Beyond: Sharing Your Feelings with Family Members

With the students, discuss some of the letters that Cassie wrote to her mother, focusing on Cassie's sense of humor. Ask students to meet with partners to discuss situations in which they want to "talk out" their feelings with someone in their family or with another adult they know.

Target Activity: A Letter to a Family Member

Based upon the above discussion, ask students to write a letter to a family member with whom they have recently experienced a conflict. Encourage students to address the issue in a positive, upbeat way, using what Cassie learned about dealing with conflict through humor. Invite the students to send their letter to the chosen family member if they feel comfortable doing so.

Sevela, Ephraim (1989). *We Were Not Like Other People.* **New York: Harper & Row.**

Heritage: Russian

Family Context:

✦ absent father

✦ community as family

✦ family adversity

Genre: historical fiction

Grades: 6+

In 1937, a nine-year-old boy loses his Red Army Commander father to Stalin's purge. The following six years are retold, in the first person, through vignettes that begin and end abruptly. At the end of the war, the boy is reunited with the other members of his family. The boy perseveres and survives the loss of his father and the devastation of the war. Good people help him overcome his obstacles and assist him during his times of great deprivation.

Discussion and Beyond: Surviving a Loss

Before discussing the story specifically, discuss the concept of surviving a loss in a family. For those students interested in this subject, suggest that they compare this story with *The Wild Children* (New York: Charles Scribner's, 1983) by Felice Holman (for grades 6–8).

Target Activity: A Reunion with Family Members

Have students imagine that they are to be part of a family reunion and must pay particular attention to inviting family members who have been away for a length of time. Engage them in planning a reunion for members of their extended family (and their friends, if appropriate). What needs to be done to prepare for the reunion? As the students respond, make a "to do" list on the chalkboard. For instance:

1. A day, time, and place needs to be selected, and relatives should be invited as guests. (Engage students in designing and making invitations and envelopes to mail the information to the guests.)

2. Different foods need to be prepared. (Engage students in making a list of the foods to be prepared; have them select one of the dishes and make a grocery list of needed ingredients.)

Suggest that the students share their invitations and list of foods with their parent(s) and offer to help with the plans for the next family reunion.

Sebestyen, Ouida (1994). *Out of Nowhere*. New York: Orchard.

Heritage: European

Family Context:

◆ absent mother

◆ family concerns

◆ intergenerational relationship

Genre: contemporary realistic fiction

Grades: 5–8

Harley Nunn realizes that he is alone in the world when his mother abandons him at an Arizona campground. There, Harley encounters a pit bull named Ish and an older woman, May, who takes them under her wing to travel to her mountain home where they meet the renter, Bill. The curious group tries to rebuild their broken lives by forming a new family together through the relationships of cooperation, forgiveness, hope, and love.

Discussion and Beyond: When You Feel Alone

With the students, discuss feeling lonely, mentioning that being "alone" is not necessarily the same as being "lonely." Have the students contribute words related to loneliness, and list the words on the chalkboard emanating from a word web with "When You Feel Alone" at the center.

Target Activity: Creating a Family

Ask students to describe what qualities made Harley's strange group a family to him. Discuss the difference between family and friendship. Have the students write a short paragraph describing how strangers entering their home would know that their family was indeed a family rather than merely a group of people living together.

PARENT-SON RELATIONSHIP

Salisbury, Graham (1992). *Blue Skin of the Sea.* **New York: Delacorte.**

Heritage: Native American
Family Context:
+ father-son relationship
+ family adversity
+ family support
Genre: contemporary realistic fiction
Grades: 7–8

On the island of Hawaii, in the village of Kailua-Kona, Sonny Mendoza and his father face the sea and their natural enemies. Sonny's difficulties in growing up are portrayed in short stories that focus on Sonny's childhood, his confrontation with a sixth-grade bully, his teenage years, his interest in a beautiful girl, and his search for his identity when his father's fishing boat fails to return to port on time and Sonny fears he has lost him.

Discussion and Beyond: Support of a Parent

With students, discuss the support Sonny's father gave him at different times. How did Sonny feel about the support his father gave him? Discuss the family ties and the difficulties Sonny faced as he grew up, and draw parallels between them. Using students' suggested words that describe how Sonny felt about the support he was given, create a web on the chalkboard with the words "Feelings of Sonny Mendoza" at the center and the students' ideas radiating from the center.

Target Activity: Family Support Book

After the above discussion, ask students to think of a time they received valuable support from a family member when they had difficulties similar to Sonny's, such as facing a bully or dealing with a jealous friend. Have students describe the incident in an essay, including how the love and support of the family members helped them work out the problem and learn from it. Have students revise their essays using peer editing. Compile the essays into a class book about the importance of family support.

Cottonwood, Joe (1992). *Danny Ain't.* **New York: Scholastic.**

Heritage: European
Family Context:
+ father-son relationship
+ family conflict
+ family crisis
+ single father

Genre: contemporary realistic fiction

Grades: 6+

When Danny's dad recovers from his post–Vietnam War trauma and leaves the hospital, he retrieves Danny from the "charity" home where Danny was placed and they move to San Puerco, California, where they barely manage to make a living and survive. His father's trauma returns, and Danny manages on his own until his father returns from the rehabilitation center. During this time alone, Danny gains from his wise decisions and suffers from his not-so-wise decisions. He turns for help to his friends; his coach; and, with a surprising prince-and-the-pauper similarity, to a wealthy boy who is overprotected. Keeping his father's absence a secret the entire time his father is away, Danny greets his father when he returns, knowing that he has grown inside a good deal. Danny is quite proud of what he "is" and what he "ain't."

Discussion and Beyond:
What You "Is" and What You "Ain't"

With the students, discuss Danny's struggle and compare what Danny goes through to the metaphor of the two coyotes, who also struggle to accommodate their lives into a world that seems increasingly dangerous and hostile. Ask the students to discuss the things Danny "is" proud of as well as some of the things Danny "ain't" proud of.

Target Activity: Who Am I?

Very often, students have a hard time separating who they are themselves from who they are within a family. On a ditto master, draw an outline of a young person and give one to each student. On one side of the outline, have students write words to describe who they are. On the other side, have students write words to describe who they are not, even though others, including family members, may think they are. Using these outlines as props, invite students to share with a partner how they hope others see them. Invite students to share their outlines with the class.

Finley, M. P. (1993). *Soaring Eagle.* **New York: Simon & Schuster.**

Heritage: Hispanic

Family Context:

✦ **father-son relationship**

✦ **family adversity**

✦ **family heritage**

Genre: historical fiction

Grades: 7–8

Rumors of war between Mexico and the United States send Julio Montoya and his father to Fort Bend. Julio, a young adolescent, comes of age in Fort Bend resenting the impending war and resisting his father's attempts to protect him from the trauma of the war. This story is best for individual reading by mature readers because of the emotional and sensitive material.

Discussion and Beyond:
Rumors of War . . .

Since 1776, many Americans have served in major wars, and some students will recall a family member's service in the armed forces. Have those students discuss the experience of the family member, focusing on how the absence of the family member was dealt with by the rest of the family.

Target Activity:
Causes and Family Reflections

Divide the class into groups of four students each. Have groups list possible reasons governments initiate wars (e.g., to help an ally, to gain land or seaports or resources, to protect or preserve their or another country, to punish a hostile country, etc.). Have the students list reasons for war from their family member's point of view. From both lists, have students check off those reasons that would make them decide to go to war. If they are opposed to war under any circumstance, ask them to write down their reasons.

Dygard, Thomas (1995). *Infield Hit.* **New York: Morrow.**

Heritage: European

Family Context:

✦ **father-son relationship**

✦ **divorce**

Genre: realistic fiction

Grades: 6–8

Hal Stevens is trying to live up to his famous father, Ralph Stevens, a former third-base superstar. Hal's parents are divorced, and Hal moves to another high school. His new coach switches him to second base and suggests he try using a lighter bat. Hal finds that he must deal with Warner Dawson, the displaced second baseman, as well as the overwhelming fear of his father's disappointment in him.

Discussion and Beyond:
Dealing with Criticism

Our parents' dreams for us are often not the same dreams we have for ourselves. Ask students if their parents or caretakers have ever expressed a hope that they would do certain things, attain certain grades, or aspire to careers that were different from their desires or talents. What conflicts, if any, did this cause, and how was it resolved? With students, brainstorm some ways they could try to explain to parents that they have different dreams and talents than those that seem to be expected of them.

Target Activity:
Filling Very Large Shoes

Ask students to choose a famous person they admire and imagine that they are the offspring of that person. Have them write a paragraph describing what it might be like to be constantly compared with this person, and how they might handle it.

Bergman, Tamar (1988). *The Boy from over There.* **Translated from Hebrew by Hilel Halkin. Boston: Houghton Mifflin.**

Heritage: Middle Eastern

Family Context:

◆ father-son relationship

◆ extended family

◆ family adversity

Genre: historical fiction

Grades: 4–6

After the war and waiting in the children's house in 1947, the children watch for the return of their fathers. The children were evacuated from their underground shelter to Yavne'el, a small town out of artillery range. Though Rina's father never returns, Rami's father comes back, accompanied by a cousin, Avramik, a boy from Israel. Avramik, as a newcomer, struggles with language and the unfamiliar ways of living on the kibbutz. With the exception of Rina, who empathizes with him for his loss of family, and Roughie, a frightened pup who attaches himself to the boy, the other children make fun of Avramik. When he acts heroically during a crisis, however, the other children change their attitude about him and begin to accept him.

Discussion and Beyond: Resolving Conflicts

Divide the class into small groups. Have them brainstorm alternative endings to the story as well as resolutions to the children's insensitivity and lack of empathy for Avramik and his loss of family. Encourage groups to share their ideas with the class.

Target Activity: Accepting a Cousin into the Family

Have students work with partners and play the role of either Rina or Avramik. Ask them to act out family situations that occurred when Avramik had to adjust to a new family life, language, and culture and Rina had to adapt to a strange, new family member competing for love, affection, and resources of the family.

Heyer, Marilee (1986). *The Weaving of a Dream: A Chinese Folktale.* **Illustrated by the author. New York: Viking.**

Heritage: Chinese

Family Context:

◆ mother-son relationship

◆ family problem solving

Genre: folk literature

Grades: 4–6

A poor widow weaves her dreams into a beautiful brocade and will die of grief if her three sons are unable to recover her treasure from the fairies who stole it. To assist their mother, the three sons do all they can to solve the problem of how to recover the stolen brocade. This is a Chinese legend with an element of magic, retold lyrically and illustrated with rich, full-page, full-color illustrations.

Discussion and Beyond: Helping a Parent Achieve Their Dream

As in much folk literature, the mother in this story had only one intense dream, and her sons were determined to do anything to help her achieve it. Ask students if they know what their parent's greatest dream is. Write their ideas on the chalkboard. Have students ask their parent whether what they imagined was correct. In class, discuss any differences between what they had imagined their parent's dream to be and what the dream actually is.

Target Activity: A Mother's Dreams

After reading the story, discuss with students the idea of thinking of all their dreams and concentrating on having their dreams all in one place. Because their dreams will include beautiful settings, ideas, and objects, suggest that a beautiful pattern can be made using cloth. Invite students to design a dream cloth with paper, crayons, paints, and colored pencils. To accompany their dream cloth, have students write a narrative to explain the meaning of their designs. Have students read aloud their narratives.

PARENT-DAUGHTER RELATIONSHIP

Henke, Kevin (1995). *Protecting Marie.* **New York: Greenwillow.**

Heritage: European

Family Context:

✦ father-daughter relationship

✦ family conflict

Genre: contemporary realistic fiction

Grades: 6–8

This realistic novel recounts the love-hate relationship that Fanny Swann has with her father, and her desire to own a dog, against her father's wishes. Even though Fanny knows that her father loves her, she fears him because he is a temperamental artist, and she does not really understand him. The title metaphorically reflects Fanny's anxiety: She transfers her needs and shields her doll, Marie. When her father brings her a dog, she painstakingly tries to keep it out of her father's way. After a particularly fearful time, when Fanny's father's temper has flaired repeatedly, Fanny finds out that she and her father are more alike than she realized.

Discussion and Beyond: Living with Ambivalence

Write the word *ambivalence* on the chalkboard. Explain the meaning of this word, and share with students that this feeling usually accompanies any deep and intense relationship, even though students sometimes erroneously believe that they should feel love, and only love, for a loved one at all times. Ask students to select a partner. Have them think of a loved one that they do not always feel positive about and orally complete the following sentence about the person: "I love you when you _____, but I don't like it when you _____."

Target Activity: Fearing a Loved One

Fanny came to realize that she misunderstood her father, and when the two finally communicated about her feelings of fear, these feelings were greatly dissipated. Ask students if there is anyone in their family whom they love very much but whom they are somewhat afraid of, just as Fanny feared her father. Ask students to write a letter to the loved one they fear, explaining in gentle terms what actions are causing them to feel fearful. Explain to students that they need not deliver the letter if they do not want to—sometimes just the act of putting their feelings into words helps them come to terms with their feelings.

McCaffrey, Anne (1976). *Dragonsong.* **New York: Atheneum.**

Heritage: European

Family Context:

✦ father-daughter relationship

✦ family conflict

Genre: fanciful fiction

Grades: 5–6

On Pern, the third planet of Rukbat (a golden star), Menolly, a young girl, fights for her dream to become a harpist. Because her father believes that such a desire is disgraceful for a female, he forbids her to play her music. Menolly runs away and makes friends with the dragons, who move by teleportation. She learns that she does not need to hide her skills or fear her desires.

Discussion and Beyond: A Confrontive Father-Daughter Situation

Discuss the feelings of Menolly when she realized that her father thought it was disgraceful for a girl to become a harpist and forbade her to play the music she loved. Ask the students to discuss any experiences in their lives (or in the lives of someone they know) in which someone wanted to follow a dream and a parent forbade it. Interested students (grades 6–8) will want to read more about Menolly in the second and third books of the series, *Dragonsinger* (New York: Atheneum, 1977) and *Dragonquest* (New York: Atheneum, 1981).

Target Activity: Following Our Dreams

Ask students to write down on a piece of paper a secret dream or longing that they have. This might be a career goal, a skill that they wish to develop, or a place that they wish to be. Have students write what they think their parents' reaction to this dream would be. (Explain that these papers will not be shared with the class; they are confidential.) Encourage students to talk to their parents about their secret dream if they have not already done so.

Langton, Jane (1980). *The Fledgling.* **Illustrated by Erik Blegvad. New York: Harper & Row.**

Heritage: European

Family Context:

◆ mother-daughter relationship

◆ family responsibilities

◆ stepfamilies

Genre: contemporary realistic fiction/fanciful fiction

Grades: 5–6

A magical adventure begins in an old house in Concord as Uncle Fred Hall, Georgie Dorian's stepfather, conducts the Concord College of Transcendental Knowledge in the nineteenth-century house. Words from Thoreau are quoted, and Georgie's stepfather models his life on the teachings of Emerson and Thoreau. Georgie's mother loves and cares for her because she understands the needs of Georgie, as well as the needs of an orphaned niece and nephew. A large Canada goose—a Goose Prince—hoots softly from the porch roof outside her window, and Georgie climbs on his back for a flight around Walden Pond. He teaches her—the fledgling—to fly, a wish she has always had. The nighttime flights and their talks come to an end when Georgie is shot by a hunter who mistakes her for a flying goose.

Discussion and Beyond: A Mother Understands Her Daughter's Needs

Ask students to think of a time when someone took good care of them, and they appreciated the care. What did they say to show their appreciation? Discuss what the Goose Prince meant when he told Georgie to take good care of the gleaming turning ball that was an image of Earth. Georgie promised with the words "I will."

Target Activity: A Broken Promise

Ask students if they have ever promised to do something for another member of the family and then forgot or, for some reason, did not follow through with the promise (it is helpful for the teacher to begin by sharing a personal incident to assure students that this has happened to everyone and is not a cause for shame or embarrassment). Invite students to relate the promise and how they felt when they realized that they had not kept the promise. If the students do not bring it up, mention the value of trust and what occurs when someone can count on and trust another's words and actions.

Hurwitz, Johanna (1982). *The Rabbi's Girls.* **Illustrated by Pamela Johnson. New York: Morrow.**

Heritage: European

Family Context:

✦ father-daughter relationship

✦ family adversity

Genre: historical fiction

Grades: 5–6

Carrie is one of the six daughters of Rabbi Levin in this story set in the early twentieth century. This rich account of a stressful year in the life of the family is told through Carrie's eyes. When her youngest sister is born, many of the women in the neighborhood worry that her father will be disappointed that this sixth child is not a son, but Carrie notices the rabbi's huge smile when he is told that he has another daughter. She realizes that the rabbi thinks that girls are just as important as boys. "If God is good," Carrie asks him, "why does He make bad things like sickness and people getting angry at one another?" Gently and wisely, her father explains that life is both bitter and good. In both happy and sad times, the rabbi's wisdom and strength are shared with Carrie as she must face prejudice and hard times. The story is important for Carrie's courage, but also for the sensitive and tender way the rabbi raises his six daughters.

Discussion and Beyond: Fathers and Daughters

Ask students why the rabbi might have been disappointed with another daughter. Survey girls in the class, asking them how they were told their fathers felt when they were born. If they are unaware of what their father's reaction to their gender was, encourage the girls to question their fathers (or another member of the family) and share what they learn with the class.

Target Activity: Daughters in Other Cultures

Encourage students to share stories that they have heard in their family about the birth of sons and daughters. Divide the class into research groups. Have groups select a country, such as China,

India, or Saudi Arabia, and investigate how families in these countries feel about the birth of sons and daughters. Have them speculate as to why sons may be favored over daughters. Discuss whether these reasons are valid, and ask students if they think such preferences still persist today.

Alexander, Sue (1983). *Natalie the Willful.* **Illustrated by Lloyd Bloom. New York: Pantheon.**

Heritage: Middle Eastern

Family Context:

◆ father-daughter relationship

◆ family crisis/family conflicts

◆ sibling relationship

Genre: contemporary realistic fiction

Grades: 6–8

When Nadia's favorite brother, Hamed, has died, her father, the Shiek Tarik, decrees that no one shall ever again utter Hamed's name. Nadia becomes increasingly angry and outraged over this decree because she cannot deal with her grief in silence. Eventually, she discovers that the hurt she feels over the loss of Hamed is eased when she talks about the events and situations associated with him—her fond memories of her brother. She shares her feelings and insights about this with others, including her father. By doing so, she helps the family members make Hamed live again in their hearts by recalling their warm memories.

Discussion and Beyond: Talking to Family Members

With students, discuss a situation in which a child's pet is gone (for whatever reason) and certain adults and children in the family feel that no one should bring up the subject or talk about the lost pet. Mention that, sometimes, a child or adult feels that they cannot cope with the grief about the pet but that the hurt can be eased when the child or adult talks to other family members about fond memories associated with the pet. Invite students to relate an experience in which the hurt was eased when they talked fondly and warmly about a lost pet.

Target Activity: Appreciating Siblings

Talk to students about the phenomenon of taking loved ones for granted. Ask if any of them has ever been upset with a sibling or other family member and wished, temporarily, that they were not around. Have them imagine that they experienced the loss of the sibling the way Nadia did. Invite them to write a short skit expressing the imaginary dialogue that might have taken place between Nadia and Hamed if he had returned.

George, Jean Craighead (1994). *Julie.* **New York: HarperCollins.**

Heritage: Native American

Family Context:

+ **father-daughter relationship**
+ **family heritage**
+ **family traditions**
+ **mixed-race family**
+ **stepfamilies**

Genre: contemporary realistic fiction

Grades: 6–8

In this sequel to *Julie of the Wolves* (see p. 115), Julie returns to her father and his new wife (a white woman) in Kangik, Alaska. She realizes that the people in her community are doing all they can to survive in a changing world. She still grieves over the death of her beloved wolf, Amaroq, and she tries to protect the surviving wolves and their pack leader in her environment by moving them closer to a food source (where they will not attack the people's musk-oxen). Eventually, her father changes his point of view about killing the wolves to protect his herd.

Discussion and Beyond: Welcoming New Family Members

Ask students how a person who is in some way different, whether racially or culturally, might be welcomed into a new family. Have students imagine Julie's family life with her new stepmother. Have them describe Julie's thoughts about her new stepmother and write a short guidebook about how children might help new stepparents feel welcome and comfortable.

Target Activity: Differences and Similarities in Families

With the students, discuss the problems Julie's family had to overcome to survive in a changing environment. On the chalkboard or a chart, create two columns, labeled "similarities" and "differences." Have students fold a sheet of paper in half to make two columns, headed with the same labels. Ask students to write and dictate all the ways that families can be the same (e.g., race, number of children) and different (e.g., philosophy, race, and number of adults present) under the appropriate headings as you record their dictation on the chalkboard or chart. Ask them to meet with partners to consider the two lists. Have them rank in the similarities list the family quality that they think is most important as #1, the next most important as #2, and the third most important as #3. As a class, invite students to offer their opinions about the most important family qualities based on their lists and rankings. Two objectives will come out of this exercise. First, it shows that families are both the same and different. Second, it helps students to consider what family qualities are most important.

Brooks, Bruce (1986). *Midnight Hour Encores.* **New York: Harper & Row.**

Heritage: European

Family Context:

✦ father-daughter relationship

✦ family conflict

✦ family problem solving

Genre: contemporary realistic fiction

Grades: 6–8

Given the name Esalen Starness Blue by her flower-child mother, Sib changed her name to Sibilance T. Spooner when she was eight years old. At sixteen, Sib is bright, mature, and intolerant. She has lived her entire life with her father, Taxi, who has fostered her intellectual growth as well as her artistic growth as a cellist. Now, however, Sib wants to meet her mother, who placed Sib in Taxi's care soon after birth because the child would not fit into her free-spirit lifestyle. Father and daughter set out for California in an old Volkswagon bus for the meeting, encountering many of Taxi's offbeat friends along the way in a poignant recreation of the '60s life Taxi once lived. Sib confronts her past and makes dramatic decisions for the future that differ from her idealistic notions of what her family should be.

Discussion and Beyond:
What a Family Should Be

Sib had very idealistic notions about what a family should be. Ask students if they ever feared that their family was not all that a family should be. Ask students if television had any effect on how they thought a family should interact. Discuss specific programs that they have watched that offered an idealistic view of what family life should be like. How are real families different? What are the most important elements in any family?

Target Activity:
Who Can Care for a Baby?

Sib's mother left her in the hands of her father because she felt she could not care for her properly. On the chalkboard or an overhead transparency, list the responsibilities of caring for a baby (e.g., changing diapers, feedings in the middle of the night, getting medical attention when the infant is sick, etc.). Ask students if a man is as capable of performing these tasks as a woman. Why? Discuss Sib's mother's decision to relinquish the rearing of her child. Did she make the right decision for Sib? Why?

Schroeder, Alan (1989). *Ragtime Tumpie.* **Illustrated by Bernie Fuchs. New York: JoyStreet/Little.**

Heritage: African American

Family Context:

✦ mother-daughter relationship

✦ family support

Genre: biography

Grades: 4–5

As a young girl, Tumpie (Josephine Baker) picks fruit from the yards and gathers coal that has fallen off the hopper cars. At night, she goes with her mother to hear ragtime music and to dance to the drums in the honky-tonks. One day, she wins a dance contest sponsored by a traveling peddler and receives a shiny silver dollar. Tumpie discovers that dancing enriches her life, and she chooses dancing as a career. (Josephine became a famous dancer in Europe in the early twentieth century.)

Discussion and Beyond:
A Different Kind of Family

With the students, emphasize cultural and family diversity, and help students realize that culture is learned. Discuss the structure of Tumpie's family and how her mother's role differed from the roles of mothers in other stories. Discuss how all family members want to satisfy certain basic needs, despite the diversity of families. Discuss Tumpie and her mother's basic needs and how they satisfied their needs differently from other families students have studied. To summarize the discussion, invite the students to generalize about family diversity, family uniqueness, and family universals.

Target Activity:
A Mother's Support

This biography underscores how a mother's support can significantly affect a child's life. Ask the students to think of a talent or an ability they possess that is encouraged by their mother (or stepmother, aunt, etc.). Have them write a letter to their mother, thanking her for her support and explaining how her encouragement has made a difference in their life.

EXTENDED FAMILY RELATIONSHIPS

Mazer, Norma Fox (1980). *Mrs. Fish, Ape, and Me, the Dump Queen.* **New York: Avon.**

Heritage: European

Family Context:

◆ extended family relationship

Genre: contemporary realistic fiction

Grades: 4–6

Living with her unattractive but loving uncle who manages the town dump, Joyce endures the scorn and ridicule of her classmates. Consequently, she builds walls around herself to resist the resultant pain, but Mrs. Fish, the "crazy" school custodian, begins to develop a caring relationship with her, and the walls begin to crumble. The power of love as an anchor in the lives of the three main characters overcomes the cruelty of Joyce's peer group.

Discussion and Beyond: Defending an Extended Family Member

Ask students to think of a time when they, or a family member, were ridiculed or scorned by a person outside the family. How did they respond?

After reading this book, would they now handle ridicule in a different way? How?

Target Activity: The Power of Love

Throughout the story, there is a focus on the power of love of a caring other, who may or may not be a family member. Discuss with students the effect of this power on the pain that Joyce suffers. With the students playing the role of Joyce, ask them to write a long note to Mrs. Fish, telling her about how she has helped Joyce control the pain she feels.

Lipsyte, Robert (1991). *The Brave.* **New York: HarperCollins.**

Heritage: Native American

Family Context:

◆ extended family

◆ family adversity

◆ mixed-race family

◆ single mother

◆ uncle-nephew relationship

Genre: contemporary realistic fiction

Grades: 7–8

Sonny Bear, the son of a white father and an Indian mother, spent his childhood moving with his mother from town to town. When his mother ran out of money, Sonny was sent to live with his Uncle Jake on the Moscondaga Reservation. Now a young man, Sonny Bear has a raging anger, which he releases ferociously when he boxes in local matches. Following his dream to be a heavyweight boxer, Sonny leaves his uncle for New York City, where his troubles begin. Hustlers steal his wallet, and in the scuffle Sonny knocks out a police officer. He is arrested for making a drug run and refuses the help from an officer who is willing to let him off the hook. After serving a prison term during which he is badly knifed, he returns to the reservation to train with his Uncle Jake for the boxing career that he wants.

Discussion and Beyond: A Family Member's Help

Discuss with students how Uncle Jake helped Sonny, before he left the reservation and after he returned. Sonny's dream was to become a heavyweight champion, and with his uncle's help, he began a series of fights leading to the Gotham Globes title, but his hopes were dashed. Ask students how Sonny felt when he was disqualified after someone tipped off the boxing commission that Sonny had been paid for fighting earlier in his career.

Target Activity: Dealing with Anger

Have students meet with partners to discuss what the phrase "ways to deal with anger" means to them. Ask them to fold a sheet of paper in half to make two columns. In the left-hand column labeled "Pluses," ask the students to list the positive ways that Sonny dealt with his anger and why this behavior was constructive. How did his friends and family react when Sonny's behavior was constructive? Have students label the right-hand column "Minuses." In this column, ask the students to list the negative ways that Sonny dealt with his anger and why this behavior was destructive. How did this behavior affect his family members and friends? Have partnerships create a list of guidelines to help themselves and others turn their anger toward positive, constructive behavior. Invite students to share with the class their guidelines for dealing with anger.

Stolz, Mary (1992). *Stealing Home*. **New York: HarperCollins.**

Heritage: European

Family Context:
+ **extended family relationships**
+ **family conflict**
+ **intergenerational relationship**

Genre: contemporary realistic fiction

Grades: 4–6

Ten-year-old Tom and Grandfather, who like to talk about baseball, let cranky Aunt Linzy, Grandfather's sister-in-law, move in with them, causing a disruption in their lives. Aunt Linzy, forced to retire, upsets the relationship when she takes over Tom's room. Grandfather becomes irritable and grumbles. The baseball words "Stealing home" becomes a code phrase for them meaning their peaceful, harmonious relationship. It is only when Aunt Linzy finds a job in another town and moves out that Tom and Grandfather can return to their bachelor lifestyle. They find themselves back in their world of fishing, playing baseball, working puzzles, and playing games that are never put away but stay spread out all the time.

Discussion and Beyond: A Wider Definition of Family

Engage students in a discussion to help them understand the problems these two bachelors experienced adjusting to the presence of Aunt Linzy. Discuss how Aunt Linzy showed Tom a wider definition of what the word *family* can mean. Divide the class into groups, and ask the students to compare the family situation in *Stealing Home* with family situations in other stories they have read. Discuss the following questions:

1. Do you know about someone who has just "joined" a family you know? What did it mean for a family to have someone new move in?

2. If you had been with Tom and Grandfather during this time, what would you have done to help them adjust to the presence of Aunt Linzy?

3. If you had been with Tom and Grandfather, would you have joined them in saying words "Stealing Home" as a metaphor for their bachelor lives? What would you have said?

Target Activity: Upsetting the Family Balance

Ask students to think of a time when a friend or relative came to visit for a short or extended period of time. How did this upset the balance of relationships in the family? Have the students write a paragraph about a time (real or imagined) when the balance in their family was upset because of a visitor. Have them include a list of "Do's and Don'ts for Family Visitors."

Burnett, Frances Hodgson (1971). *The Secret Garden.* Illustrated by Tasha Tudor. New York: Dell.

Heritage: English

Family Context:

+ extended family (cousins)
+ family support
+ uncle-niece relationship

Genre: historical fiction

Grades: 4–6

This children's classic was first published in 1911 but contains universal appeal for readers in the 1990s. Mary, a contrary little orphan, comes from India to live with her cold, unfeeling uncle on the windswept English moors after her parents die of cholera. Wandering the grounds of her uncle's immense manor house one day, Mary discovers a secret garden, locked and abandoned. This event sparks a series of discoveries—her uncle's invalid child hidden within the mansion, her first friendship, and her true self. Mary begins to reach out to her caretakers, and they change from custodians into members of a family, replete with love and commitment.

Discussion and Beyond: Changing the Attitudes of Family Members

Mary, the young orphan in the story, was initially a sour, selfish child who repelled those around her. With students, discuss how Mary kept those around her at a distance when she first came to live at Mistlethwaite. Have students enumerate the things she did that drew those around her closer to her until they became a real family. Ask students to reflect upon what behaviors they could display that would help them unify their families.

Target Activity:
Mary, Before and After

Using the vivid description of Mary when she first came to live with her uncle on the moors, and description of Mary after several months of living among a nurturing family, have the students draw "before" and "after" pictures. Using the pictures as a prop, have students explain how the love and support of a caring new family helped Mary bloom.

Aesop (1981). "The Town Mouse and the Country Mouse." In *Aesop's Fables*, selected and illustrated by Heidi Holder. New York: Viking.

Heritage: European

Family Context:
✦ extended family relationship
✦ family diversity

Genre: folk literature

Grades: 4–5

The Country Mouse invited his cousin, the Town Mouse, to dinner and gave him the best food. The Town Mouse disliked the food and said, "How can you stand such food? Why don't you come home with me?" When they arrived in the city, the Town Mouse gave him nuts, dates, cake, and fruit, and saw a huge creature dash into the room with a terrible roar. He made up his mind to go home and said, "I'd rather have common food in safety than dates and nuts in the midst of danger."

Discussion and Beyond:
Different Lifestyles

Ask students if they have any cousins or other relatives who have lifestyles that are markedly different from theirs. Ask them to describe the differences and discuss why one lifestyle may not necessarily be better or worse than another—simply different.

Target Activity:
Country Family and City Family

Divide the class into small groups. Ask each group to write a short skit based upon "The Town Mouse and the Country Mouse," in which a family with a particular lifestyle (e.g., they live in the city, they love the outdoors, or they enjoy teasing one another) visits their relatives, a family with an entirely different lifestyle (e.g., they live in the country, they never go outside, or they are very serious and formal with one another). Have groups present their skits to the rest of the class. After the skits, discuss the importance of being open to and accepting of the differences of diverse families.

ADOPTION

Lowry, Lois (1989). *Number the Stars.* **Boston: Houghton Mifflin.**

Heritage: Danish

Family Context:

✦ adoption

✦ family crisis

✦ sibling relationship

Genre: historical fiction

Grades: 4–6

By 1943, ten-year-old Annemarie Johansen was accustomed to the Nazi soldiers who had been on every corner of Copenhagen for three years as she walked to school with her little sister and her best friend, Ellen Rosen. Like the lack of meat and butter, the soldiers were a nuisance of the war. Suddenly one night, Ellen comes to live with her as a sister, and the older Rosens are hidden by the resistance. Late that night, Nazi soldiers awaken them and demand to know where the Rosens are. Before the girls get out of bed, Annemarie breaks Ellen's gold chain and hides her Star of David. After searching the apartment, the Nazis ask why one daughter has dark hair. Quickly, the father goes to the family picture album and rips out three baby pictures to show to the Nazis, carefully obscuring the dates of birth. One picture shows Annemarie's older sister, now dead, who was born with dark hair. With this invasion into their home, the girls realize that the Nazis are no longer just a nuisance.

Discussion and Beyond: Having a New Sister or Brother in the Family

Discuss with the students the event when Annemarie's Lutheran family learned that the Nazis were about to relocate Denmark's 7,000 Jews, including the Rosens, the family who lived in the same apartment building. Elicit from the students how they would have felt if they had been there. What would they have said and done when a faux brother or sister, like Ellen Rosen, arrived to live with them during troubling times. Invite students to relate this experience to contemporary times and share with the class a time when someone lived with their family as another "brother" or "sister." Have them share how they helped make the newcomer feel a part of the family.

Target Activity: Families Courageous in War

Mention to students that the destructive force of war has always been present in human life, in all time periods, and that humans have always persevered. Emphasize this idea by reading selected scenes from books with similar themes but different time settings and inviting the students to imagine going back in time to discover the destructive force of war and its effects on people from other time periods. To counter the disheartening thoughts about war, call attention to the heroes and heroines who also emerge from such desolate eras. Have students read newspapers and magazines for stories about the exceptional valor that men and women have shown in times of war, such as the bravery of those selfless persons who helped the Jews escape during World War II.

McGraw, E. J. (1953). *Mara, Daughter of the Nile*. New York: Coward.

Heritage: Egyptian

Family Context:

✦ adoption

✦ homelessness

Genre: historical fiction

Grades: 6–8

During the rule of Hatshepsut, Mara, a young slave, tries to escape and is bought by a man who offers her luxury if she will spy for the queen. Mara also sells her services as a spy for the king to a young nobleman, Lord Sheftu. Eventually, her love for Sheftu changes her from a spy into a selfless heroine who endures torture rather than betray her loyalties to her new family.

Discussion and Beyond: New 'Family'

Ask students to discuss the differences between Mara's situation of being brought into a family group and the situation of adoption. How are the two situations of being "chosen" different? As an older child, what were Mara's options in this ancient time period? How did she make the best of a bad situation?

Target Activity: Loyalties to Your Family

Mara was willing to endure torture to stay with her beloved new family. Invite students to write a paragraph stating what they would be willing to do to protect and maintain their families. Encourage students to illustrate their paragraph by portraying all members of their family and themselves performing a heroic deed to rescue their family.

Willis, Patricia (1991). *A Place to Claim as Home*. New York: Clarion.

Heritage: European

Family Context:

✦ adoption

✦ diverse families

✦ family support

Genre: historical fiction

Grades: 6–8

In Ohio in 1943, thirteen-year-old Henry and middle-aged Sarah are thrown together by chance when Henry, an orphan, is placed with Sarah on her farm for the summer. Over the course of the summer, the two independent but lonely people begin to care for each other and have the courage to admit it. They realize that they can be, in a very real sense, a family. Although this story is not about World War II, the effects of the war are visible and portrayed realistically.

Discussion and Beyond: What Is a Family?

Sarah and Henry come together and become, in their words, "a family." Ask students what are the minimum requirements for calling a group of people "a family." What is the difference between several friends living together and the relationship that Henry and Sarah shared? Have students look up the word *family* in the dictionary and compare that definition with their definition.

Target Activity: A Celebration of Diverse Families

Have students imagine a family that differs from so-called traditional families (the family can be theirs, a family they know, a family they know about, or fictional). Ask students to illustrate the members of this family, describe each member, and explain the traits that make this collection of people a family. Display the products of this endeavor on a class bulletin board titled "A Celebration of Diverse Families."

Murphy, Barbara B. (1994). *Fly Like an Eagle.* **New York: Delacorte.**

Heritage: Native American

Family Context:

✦ adoption

✦ extended family

✦ family heritage

✦ father-son relationship

Genre: contemporary realistic fiction

Grades: 7–8

On an across-the-country search for his family's roots, Barney, a father who was adopted, and his son, Ace, drive from New York City to an Ohio orphanage and, from there, to Kansas City, where Barney Hobart's birth grandmother lives. The eccentric woman, a former trapeze artist, and her twin sister tell Barney that his birth father is a Pueblo Indian, and the two drive on to New Mexico. When they meet their lost relatives, they are received warmly and initiated into the clan.

Discussion and Beyond: Searching for One's Roots

Ask students why Barney was interested in learning more about his roots. Was Barney surprised by what he learned? How did the newfound knowledge help and hinder him? Why might adopted children be interested in searching for their birth parents? How might their adoptive families feel about the search?

Target Activity: Two Different Families

Barney grew up in a white, middle-class family and then discovered that his relatives belonged to a Native American tribe. He then, effectively, had two very different family groups. Discuss this with students, and ask them to meet in small groups to list the advantages and disadvantages of trying to be accepted into two different families—and two different worlds. Invite students who have been adopted or who know of adopted relatives who searched and found their birth parents to further clarify the advantages and disadvantages of having two families.

Nixon, Joan Lowery (1989). *Caught in the Act. New York: Bantam.*

Heritage: European

Family Context:

✦ adoption

✦ abusive parent

Genre: historical fiction

Grades: 4–6

Eleven-year-old Mike Kelly lives with Mr. and Mrs. Friedrich in a foster home environment. Unfortunately, Mr. Friedrich wants to break Mike of his "evil city ways" with beatings, and Mr. Friedrich's son, Gunter, dislikes Mike so much that he makes it seem like Mike has been lying and stealing. The social services agency learns of the abuse and mistreatment and sends Mike to live with a new family.

Discussion and Beyond: How Could I Behave?

With the students, discuss how Gunter Friedrich shows that he disliked Mike Kelly. In each situation,

how did Mike respond to Gunter? After discussion, invite the students to make a list of the ways they could show their friendship to a foster child in their home. The list might be titled "How I Could Behave."

Target Activity: Reporting Abuse

Invite a representative from a social services agency in your area to talk to the class about reporting abuse (e.g., what exactly constitutes child abuse, how children should handle it, and who they should talk to about it). Before the visit, invite the students to consider questions they might like to ask the representative—in regard to their family life and in regard to Mike Kelly's family life.

Conflicts Within Families

FAMILY ADVERSITY

Matas, Carol (1987). *Lisa's War.* **New York: Scribner's.**

Heritage: Danish

Family Context:

◆ family adversity

◆ family support

◆ sibling relationship

Genre: historical fiction

Grades: 6+

Set in Copenhagen during World War II, this novel is based on true experiences. Lisa and her brother, Stefan, Jewish teenagers, join the organized resistance movement to stop the Nazis from sending Jews to concentration camps. Lisa and Stefan warn friends and neighbors to flee to coastal towns and escape to neutral Sweden in the fall of 1943, before a roundup of Danish Jews by the Nazis. In Denmark, Lisa perseveres and helps the resistance movement: She surreptitiously distributes anti-Nazi literature on streetcars and, with her friend Suzanne, performs life-threatening jobs for the resistance.

Discussion and Beyond: Sibling Heroes

Discuss the heroic acts performed by Lisa, Stefan, and Suzanne in this historical novel. Ask students to speculate as to how Lisa's strong relationship with her brother gave her the courage to perform such

noble deeds during the war. Ask students to contribute examples of siblings who behaved courageously with each other's support. Students may refer to stories they have read, informational text, newspaper articles, or incidents reported on television.

Target Activity: Family Problems in Times of War

The story emphasizes the heroics of battling against enemies, the tragedies of war, and life-threatening situations. Because these events are common to all wars, other books can be used to further discussion about family problems in times of war. Consider reading aloud short excerpts from *Across Five Aprils* (for grades 4–6) by Irene Hunt (New York: Follett, 1964), set during the Civil War era, and *Johnny Tremain* (for grades 4–6) by Esther Forbes (Boston: Houghton Mifflin, 1943), set during the Revolutionary War. Using details from the excerpts, have students create journal entries about times of war.

Bunting, Eve (1996). *Dandelions.* **New York: Harcourt Brace.**

Heritage: European

Family Context:

✦ family adversity

Genre: historical fiction

Grades: 4–6

This is a story of a family moving from Illinois to Nebraska during the westward migrations in the United States during the mid-1800s. They travel across the plains in a covered wagon pulled by oxen. The father is searching for a better life and opportunities for his family. The wife and two daughters are experiencing the emotions of leaving home, of leaving extended family, friends, and many memories behind. The dandelions are a metaphor for this family that endures the hardship of change and yet continues trying to build a better life.

Discussion and Beyond:
Parents Sacrificing for a Better Life

Ask students to interview their parents to determine if they have ever moved, lived without certain material possessions, or in other ways sacrificed so that their family could eventually have a better life. As a class, encourage students to share the sacrifices that their parents have made. What statements do such sacrifices make about each family and the parents' commitment to their children?

Target Activity:
A Hardship Metaphor

Discuss the dandelion metaphor in this story. Ask students to write a short story about a hardship their family has endured, selecting an original metaphor to use as a unifying theme in the story. Students may use, instead, the examples of sacrifice their parents told them about in the interview for the above discussion. Have students share their family hardship stories in small groups.

Wolf, Bernard (1978). *This Proud Land: The Story of a Mexican American Family.* **New York: Lippincott.**

Heritage: Hispanic

Family Context:

✦ family adversity

✦ family heritage

Genre: historical fiction

Grades: 6–8

Traveling from the Rio Grande Valley to Minnesota to find work, the proud Hernandez family is portrayed through their relationships at work and at play as they create a better life for themselves in difficult times. The author focuses on the "many Americas" in this proud land and writes: "There is an America of inequality and racial prejudice. There is an America of grave poverty, despair, and tragic human waste. And yet because of people like the Hernandez family, there is also an America of simple courage, strength, and hope."

Discussion and Beyond:
A Better Life

Write the following at the center of the chalkboard: "Families in all time periods have tried to create a better life for themselves." Ask students to suggest examples, and record the examples radiating from the main idea to make a web. Focus students' attention on the story of the Hernandez family, and engage them in discussing its literary elements (e.g., theme, plot, author's purpose, writing style, characters, setting, authentic background).

Target Activity:
A Family Autobiography

Ask students to consider how their family has helped make America a better place. Have them write a chapter for an "autobiography," including family members and information such as

1. family heritage

2. family traditions

3. ways the family plays together

4. work done by family members

5. problems the family has faced together

6. the family's hopes and dreams

Roop, Peter, and Connie Roop (1992). *Ahyoka and the Talking Leaves.* New York: Lothrop, Lee & Shepard.

Heritage: Native American

Family Context:

◆ family adversity

◆ family support

◆ father-daughter relationship

Genre: historical fiction

Grades: 4–5

Ahyoka was the daughter of Sequoyah, and she helped him develop a written Cherokee language in the early 1800s. When he was accused of "magic" and ostracized from the tribe, Ahyoka supported him, and they left together. She helped discover that letters could be related to sounds, which was the key to the development of the Cherokee's syllabic alphabet. The language was called the "talking leaves."

to record the sounds of the Cherokee language. Ask the students if they have ever worked with one of their family members to achieve a special goal or finish a certain project. Invite the students to share their experiences in small groups. As a class, have students suggest how families can work together. Write the suggestions in a list on the chalkboard under the heading "Working Together in a Family."

Discussion and Beyond:
Working Together in a Family

Discuss how Sequoyah and Ahyoka worked together to achieve something special—they tried

Target Activity:
Mural of Family Support

After the above discussion, have students make a class mural illustrating the ways they have helped family members on a recent project. Using butcher paper and tempera paints, have the students portray their family working together. Tape the butcher paper on the wall in the classroom and allocate a small space for each student. Instruct them to sketch their ideas first. During an open house or other occasion at which parents are present, encourage students to share their section of the mural, explaining how they have helped their families, just as Ahyoka did.

Collins, David R. (1990). *Tales for Hard Times: A Story About Charles Dickens.* **Illustrated by David Mataya. New York: Carolrhoda.**

Heritage: European

Family Context:

✦ **family adversity**

Genre: biography

Grades: 4–8

This life story describes how Dickens managed to leave his impoverished past behind him but chose not to forget it—Dickens made references to his past in some of his stories. For example, he had an unhappy childhood living with a father deeply in debt (who was sent to debtors' prison in London). Dickens was put to work in a warehouse, pasting labels on bottles. This unhappy experience later surfaced in *David Copperfield*, an account of Dickens's experiences during these warehouse days told through the suffering of little David. His father's experience with debtors' prison was made famous in *Little Dorrit*. In *Oliver Twist*, Dickens exposed the abuses of children in the workhouse system. *Nicholas Nickleby* tells of the severe punishment that children received in schools at the time.

Discussion and Beyond: Children's Family Responsibilities Long Ago

With students, list the jobs and family responsibilities children had in Dickens's time, as referenced in Charles Dickens's work. For comparison, make a list of chores that students do as part of their family responsibilities. In which era would they prefer to live? Why was family life so much more difficult for children in Dickens's time?

Target Activity: Dickens's Family Life in Hard Times

Discuss Dickens's childhood, and ask students to share how they managed to live through a "hard time" in the past. Have students write a short biographical paragraph about the hard times in their family life and how they managed to cope with them. As a class, ask students to explain how their hard times compare with those of Dickens's characters.

Blackwood, Alan (1987). *Beethoven.* **New York: Bookwright.**

Heritage: European

Family Context:

✦ family adversity

✦ sibling relationships

Genre: biography

Grades: 4–6

Ludwig van Beethoven's life story was one of struggle and disappointment. He began composing music at age eleven and was an assistant court organist in Bonn at age fourteen. After his mother died in 1787, Beethoven supported his brothers and sisters by giving music lessons. After providing this service, he went on with his musical studies.

Discussion and Beyond: Helping Your Family

Engage interested students in discussing how Beethoven assisted his family. How did Beethoven feel about supporting his family? How did his brothers and sisters feel? How do the students help

their family? How do they feel when they help others? How have others shown them that they appreciate the help?

Target Activity: Showing Appreciation

Have students close their eyes and think about a sibling or other family member who has done something for them, or who is always there for them when they have a problem. Ask students to plan a way to show this family member how much they are appreciated: by making a present, writing a poem or letter, doing a special errand or chore, taking a walk together, talking together, and so on. Ask students to share with the class the outcome of their special show of appreciation.

Blair, David Nelson (1992). *Fear the Condor.* **New York: Lodestar.**

Heritage: Bolivian

Family Context:

✦ family adversity

✦ absent father

✦ family heritage

✦ family problem solving

Genre: historical fiction

Grades: 5–8

This book presents a vignette from Central American history in the 1930s. In Bolivia, the Aymara-speaking Masuru people are sharecroppers, and the Spanish-speaking patron conscripts the men

to fight for Bolivia. Ten-year-old Bartolina watches her father leave and, with the women and other girls, works twice as hard without the men. She sees her ancient society move toward a contemporary one as she learns inkweaving (reading and writing); sees labor unions form; and supports her people, who stand up for the right to own their land.

Discussion and Beyond: "Changes That Affect Family Life"

Invite the students, in partnerships, to discuss the changes that affected Bartolina's family life. Ask them to make a list from their discussion titled: "Changes That Affected Bartolina's Family Life." Invite the students to read aloud some of the entries from their list in a class discussion.

Target Activity: "Standing Up for Your Rights"

Long before Bartolina supported her people when they stood up for the right to own their land, people in America's early colonies wrote an open proclamation to all colonists, calling upon them to "stand up" for what they believed in and to tell others they were "cutting" their political ties to England. The proclamation, completed in 1776, was the Declaration of Independence, which declares that certain truths are "self-evident." Bring a copy of the Declaration of Independence to show the children. Read the preamble. Ask students to meet with partners and discuss whether they would have risked their lives and property by signing the proclamation. What other options might they have had?

Whitmore, Arvella (1990). *The Bread Winner.* **Boston: Houghton Mifflin.**

Heritage: European

Family Context:

✦ family adversity

✦ family responsibility

✦ family support

✦ two-parent family

Genre: historical fiction

Grades: 5–7

During the Great Depression, twelve-year-old Sarah uses her prizewinning bread recipe to make bread. She sells the bread and helps her family survive economic hardship that could lead to separation. Though the book highlights the life of Sarah and her family, it also shows the unfortunate repercussions of the rampant poverty of this historic time on the country and, in particular, on Sarah's community. Many families with members who were particularly resourceful, as Sarah was, found ways to eke out a meager existence.

Discussion and Beyond: Helping Out at Home

Discuss with students how Sarah used her baking talents to help out the family in a time of adversity. Invite students to brainstorm how they might be able to help out their families, using their talents, in times of economic hardship.

Target Activity: How Can a Family Survive Economic Hardship?

Ask students to research the family chores of women and girls during the nineteenth century. Discuss with students what it would be like to live during this time period, and whether or not they would want to. Ask the students if they would want to work like twelve-year-old Sarah did to help their family survive economic hardship. Do they have (or know anyone who has) a "prizewinning" bread recipe that they could use?

Uchida, Yoshiko (1978). *Journey Home.* New York: Atheneum.

Heritage: Japanese American

Family Context:

✦ family adversity

✦ family support

✦ family tradition and heritage

Genre: historical fiction

Grades: 4–6

This story poignantly describes the painful experience of the Japanese living in America during World War II, seen through the eyes of Yuki, a Japanese American girl. Yuki and her mother and father are released from a concentration camp in the Utah desert and return to Berkeley, where they lived before the war. Woven into this story is a tragic theme of discrimination against Yuki's Japanese family and a host of misunderstandings, made bearable only by the support of her loving family. Yuki and her family eventually come to terms with their captors after the war, as mistrust gives way to forgiveness.

Discussion and Beyond: The Effect of Internment on a Family

Ask students to imagine that they and their family have been arrested in the middle of the night and brought to a concentration camp, for no good reason. How would they and their family members react? What strategies would help them cope with this experience? What strategies did Yuki's family use? Did this experience bring Yuki's family closer together?

Target Activity: Family Support During Difficult Times

In groups of four, have students do the following activity:

1. Review the situation of Yuki's family during their internment.

2. Discuss the effect of internment on families and the arguments for and against the internment of Japanese families during this time period.

3. To help children internalize the complexity of these arguments, involve them in a role play of the trial scene from the book. Decide who in the group will role play the parts of a family member; a defense attorney, who will defend the government; and a prosecuting attorney, who will defend the family.

4. After discussing the role play, ask the students to write the headings "argument" and "counterargument" on paper.

5. Have students write their arguments on paper as a group and then trade papers with another group. Ask the groups to counterargue the arguments on the paper they received.

Taylor, Mildred (1976). *Roll of Thunder, Hear My Cry.* **Illustrated by Jerry Pinkney. New York: Dial.**

Heritage: African American

Family Context:

✦ family adversity

✦ family problem solving

Genre: historical fiction

Grades: 4–6

All the members of the Logan family have an allegiance to the land, which they have owned since Reconstruction days. However, for nine-year-old Cassie the land seems to have been a source of constant conflict and upheaval in her family. She wishes to move to a more peaceful place. Cassie sees the night riders who terrorize her community; reacts to the loss of her mother's teaching job as a result of her mother's participation in a store boycott whose owner is one of the riders; and takes pride in her father, who helps rescue a black teenager, T. J., from a lynch mob.

Discussion and Beyond: Cassie's Family and Its Problems

With students, discuss the following questions:

1. Do you know anyone whose family has lived on the same land for several generations? Why and how did Cassie's family take pride in the land they owned?

2. If you had been with Cassie and her family during this difficult time, what would you have done?

3. Would you have joined Cassie's mother as she participated in the store boycott? What would you have done?

4. Would you have joined Cassie's father as he participated in the rescue of T. J.? What would you have done?

Target Activity: Family Pride in Overcoming Adversity

Ask students to think of something a parent has done that made them feel proud of their family. (If they are unable to think of anything immediately, urge them to have a family discussion about a time when adults in the immediate or extended family stood up for their rights.) Using computer software, create blank awards for students. Have them write the name of their parent on the award along with a few words explaining the nature of the award (e.g., for standing up to your boss; for writing a letter to the editor of the paper, etc.). Encourage students to present the award to their parent and then share with the class how the recipient reacted.

Armstrong, William (1969). *Sounder.* **Illustrated by James Barkley. New York: Harper & Row.**

Heritage: African American

Family Context:

✦ family adversity

✦ absent father

✦ family member with a physical disability

Genre: historical fiction

Grades: 6–8

A black sharecropper, a father and husband, is caught stealing meat from a white man's smokehouse to feed his hungry family. He is arrested and taken away. His protective dog, Sounder, leaps at the sheriff's wagon where his master is chained. One of the men shoots the dog, leaving him disfigured and crippled, and without the spirit for barking. When the father receives a sentence of working on a gang, his wife endures, and each year his son searches for him after the crops are in. Taking place in the South with unnamed characters, *Sounder* portrays courage and human dignity, as well as tragedy and cruelty.

Discussion and Beyond: Hungry Families

In this story, the boy's father stole meat from a smokehouse to feed his hungry family. Discuss this incident with the students. Did the man want to steal? What else might he have done? Share with the students the fact that the poverty rate for black children is currently more than three times that for white children (source: The Children's Defense Fund). Is this fair? What can be done about it? Is it ever right to steal to feed hungry children? Ask students to support their answers with examples.

Target Activity: Letter of Gratitude

The boy in this story received moral support from an elderly friend. Ask students to think of an older person in their life who has been especially helpful when no one in their family would listen. Ask students to write a letter of gratitude to this person who is a "significant other" in their life. Encourage them to mail their letter, if desired.

Collier, James Lincoln (1987). *Louis Armstrong.* **New York: Macmillan.**

Heritage: African American

Family Context:

✦ **family adversity**

✦ **community as family**

Genre: biography

Grades: 4–6

In this true story, Collier tells how Louis Armstrong overcame poverty to become a jazz expert. As an example of his economic hardships, Louis was so poor growing up in New Orleans that he did not have his own trumpet until he was seventeen. The gifted musician struggled against inconceivable odds to become one of the greatest jazz trumpeters of all time.

Discussion and Beyond: What is Poverty?

Ask students to define poverty. How did Louis Armstrong achieve such great success in his life after growing up so poor? Have students reread the text to find ways Armstrong's family and community provided love and support, helping him succeed despite overwhelming odds.

Target Activity: Armstrong's Family Life in New Orleans

Encourage interested students to design a monument that could be built in honor of Louis Armstrong and how he and his family overcame adversity. Ask students to prepare a speech to be given at the dedication. Have students revise their speech using peer editing.

DIVORCE

Magorian, Michelle (1992). *Back Home.* **New York: Harper Trophy.**

Heritage: European

Family Context:

✦ divorce/separation

✦ absent father

✦ family conflict

Genre: historical fiction

Grades: 6+

Leaving America after World War II, Rusty Dickinson, a twelve-year-old, returns to her home in England. She finds it difficult to fit back into the rigid English way of life at her miserable boarding school with its silly rules and snobby girls. The atmosphere becomes more intolerable for Rusty when her father returns home from the war and, like Rusty's snobby grandmother, decides that Rusty should stay at the boarding school. Rusty rebels by running away. When her mother finds her and tells her that she and Rusty's father are separating, Rusty realizes that a new life is about to begin for her, her brother, and her mother.

Discussion and Beyond: Intolerable Situations

There have always been children who are miserable in their family situations. To help students gain further insight into the thoughts of everyone involved in an intolerable situation, ask students the following questions:

1. Why was Rusty Dickinson unhappy with the boarding school?

2. What do you imagine Rusty's relationship with her snobby grandmother was like?

3. Why did Rusty's father want Rusty to stay at the boarding school?

Target Activity: Alternative Endings

Divide students into groups to role play the following incidents. Have groups present alternative endings to the problems Rusty faced.

1. Rusty's snobby grandmother wanted Rusty to attend a boarding school with snobby girls and silly rules. What might Rusty say about this to a friend? How might she look and act?

2. When Rusty's father returned home from World War II, he, too, wanted her to return to the boarding school. What might Rusty have said to her father when he told her this? How might she look and act?

3. What might Rusty have said to herself as she was feeling rebellious and deciding to run away? How might she look and act? What might Rusty have said to her mother when she was found? How might she look and act?

4. What might Rusty have said to her mother when she heard that she and her father were separating? How might she look and act?

Howe, James (1987). *Carol Burnett: The Sound of Laughter.* **Illustrated by Robert Masheris. New York: Viking/Kestrel.**

Heritage: European

Family Context:

◆ divorce

◆ alcoholism

◆ intergenerational relationship

Genre: biography

Grades: 4–6

Carol Burnett grew up shuttled between her grandmother, who was on welfare and lived in a one-room apartment, and her parents, both alcoholics, who divorced when she was very young. Though she felt she was far from beautiful, she longed to become a great actress. She spent much of her time at the movies or putting on plays. She learned that by laughing at herself she could help others laugh at themselves, and she eventually became one of America's favorite comediennes. Carol Burnett's early home life was not often funny, but she put to use her mother's favorite saying, "Comedy is tragedy plus time," to create her style of comedy. She believed it was better to laugh than to cry, and she helped her audiences see that, too.

Discussion and Beyond: Making a Good Family Situation out of a Bad One

Discuss with the students how Carol Burnett used laughter to make unhappy situations into positive situations. Share an experience from your life when you used humor in this way, and invite students to share an experience when they used laughter to make a bad situation into a better situation.

Target Activity: Comedy Routines

Read to students the story of *Alexander and the Terrible, Horrible, No Good, Very Bad Day*, by Judith Viorst (New York: Dell, 1972) about a boy who, unlike Carol Burnett, doesn't know how to laugh at bad luck and becomes a victim. Discussing the events one at a time, brainstorm how Carol Burnett might have made these bad situations into hilarious comedy routines. Divide the class into groups of three or four students each. Have groups pick their favorite events from the book and create humorous sketches to perform for the class.

Feuer, Elizabeth (1995). *Lost Summer.* **New York: Farrar, Straus & Giroux.**

Heritage: European

Family Context:

◆ divorce

◆ sibling relationships

◆ absent father

Genre: realistic fiction

Grades: 6–8

Lydia Ayles and her older sister, Gina, go to camp for a summer while their divorced mother seeks further education in Italy. Lydia, confused about her father's absence, is pulled into relationships with two girls who dislike each other, requiring her to make difficult choices. In the end, Lydia learns painful truths about relationships among friends and family. Children of divorced parents will relate to the gamut of feelings that Lydia experiences, from her jealousy of her friend's happy family to her anger and hurt because of her father's seeming apathy toward her.

Discussion and Beyond: When a Parent Does Not Seem to Care

Discuss why Lydia felt that her father no longer cared about her after her parents' divorce. Ask if any students in the class whose parents went through a divorce experienced similar feelings. Encourage these students to share how they felt. Solicit ideas as to what a parent might have been going through or feeling that would make it seem like they did not really care when, in fact, they did.

Target Activity: A Happy Family

As an outside assignment, ask students to watch a television program that includes a "stereo-typical" family. In an essay, have them critique the "believability" of this family. What is not realistic about the family? How does the family differ from theirs? When all students have completed the assignment, read the critiques as part of a discussion about why many children, like Lydia, begin to believe that everyone's family except theirs is perfect and happy.

FAMILY CONFLICT

=====

Holland, Irene (1988). *Heads You Win, Tails I Lose.* **Philadelphia: Lippincott.**

Heritage: European

Family Context:

◆ family conflict

◆ absent father

◆ alcoholism

Genre: contemporary realistic fiction

Grades: 6+

Teenage Melissa is overweight and caught in the marital difficulties of her sparring parents. Her father, who appears to have a mistress, belittles Melissa, and her mother seems to feel that Melissa is the source of all her troubles. Her desire to be in a stage production, and the encouragement of a teacher and a young boy, motivate Melissa to lose weight, but her attempt is misguided—she begins taking her mother's diet pills. Her father leaves them; her mother begins drinking even more heavily; and Melissa finally realizes that, ultimately, life's journey is taken alone. She stops taking pills and goes to see her father to get help for her mother. With her burgeoning maturity, Melissa begins to understand and appreciate her family members for who they are. The pace in this story is swift, and the dialogue is appropriately tart, lending important effect.

Discussion and Beyond: What Do Families Look Like?

Ask several students to share who they think they look like in their family, and why. Ask students if it is important to have physical traits in common with family members. Why? Ask students to brainstorm how one could know whether people are related or just friends.

Target Activity: Nobody's Perfect

Melissa finally began to love her parents for who they were, despite their flaws. Ask students to think of a family member who has a problem that may or may not be one of those mentioned in this story. Ask them to write a tribute to this family member, concentrating on their positive virtues while setting aside the problem. Have them title the essay "Nobody's Perfect." Students might prefer to keep this tribute confidential, or they may want to share it with the family member.

=====

Staples, Suzanne Fisher (1989). *Shabanu.* **New York: Knopf.**

Heritage: Pakistani

Family Context:

◆ family conflict

◆ family support

Genre: contemporary realistic fiction

Grades: 6–8

Eleven-year-old Shabanu lives with her nomadic family in the desert of contemporary Pakistan. When her parents betroth her to a middle-aged man, she faces the dilemma of obeying her family or obeying her desire for well-being. Shabanu faces her inner turmoil courageously and, in doing so, finds signs of the love and warmth in her family.

Discussion and Beyond: This Is Whom You Will Marry!

Have students imagine that they are their current age and their parents have suddenly chosen a marriage partner for them. When they meet their "betrothed," they are repulsed and unhappy. How would they handle this family conflict? What would they do and say? How could they face such a situation and still keep peace in the family and within themselves?

Target Activity: Different Cultures— Different Marriage Arrangements

Divide the class into groups. Have each group select an unfamiliar culture and research courtship and marriage rituals and customs in that culture. Have students present their findings to the rest of the class including the answers to the following questions: What purposes do these customs serve? Why do these customs prevail?

Cole, Norma (1990). *The Final Tide.* New York: McElderry.

Heritage: European

Family Context:
✦ family conflict
✦ family crisis
✦ intergenerational relationship

Genre: historical fiction

Grades: 4–8

In 1948 in Tennessee, the dam built by the Tennessee Valley Authority nears completion. Soon the water will flood the valley where fourteen-year-old Geneva and her family have lived their entire lives. Geneva tries to convince her grandmother (who is determined to stay) to put down her shotgun and relocate before the water floods the valley.

Discussion and Beyond: Persuading Family Members

With the students, discuss the value of persuasive speaking and writing. Pair students together to develop arguments that Geneva could have used to convince her grandmother to relocate before the flood waters came into the valley. Ask groups to read aloud their arguments, and discuss the persuasiveness of the suggestions as a class.

Target Activity: Intergenerational Dialogue

Have students, working in partnerships, write a dialogue between Geneva and her grandmother as the young girl tries to persuade her grandmother to leave their home. Have them focus on the following aspects of having a successful dialogue, aspects that will be helpful in future intergenerational conflicts:

- Be fair.
- Present the facts logically.
- Listen to the other person's point of view.
- Be courteous.
- Try to understand how the other person is feeling.

Snyder, Zilpha Keatley (1987). *And Condors Danced.* New York: Delacorte.

Heritage: European

Family Context:

◆ family conflict

◆ aunt-niece relationship

◆ family member with a physical disability

◆ sibling relationship

Genre: contemporary realistic fiction

Grades: 5–8

Eleven-year-old Carly lives on a ranch in California with her older brothers and sister, an invalid mother, and a stern father. To find a place for herself in this difficult family, she spends much of her time with her grandaunt and rides out into the wild country with her beloved dog.

Discussion and Beyond: All for One and One for All

Ask students to discuss the traits of all the members of Carly's family. Does her family sound like the ideal family that is so often portrayed on television sitcoms? Ask students to discuss whether television families are more or less realistic than real-life families. Invite students to offer examples of how family members are not all bad or all good but three-dimensional human beings, and how students love family members unconditionally.

Target Activity: Sharing Your Feelings with a Caring Family Member

With the students, discuss some of the times that Carly spent with her great aunt and how Carly tried to find her niche among the stressful relationships. Ask students to group together in partnerships to discuss a situation in which they wanted to share their feelings with a caring member of their family or with another caring adult they know. After the discussion, engage the students in reflecting about this situation in a diary entry. Have students record their thoughts about ways they have tried to find their niche among stressful family relationships.

Speare, Elizabeth (1958). *The Witch of Blackbird Pond.* Boston: Houghton Mifflin.

Heritage: European

Family Context:

◆ family conflict

◆ extended family

◆ intergenerational relationship

Genre: historical fiction

Grades: 6+

Kit Tyler, a high-spirited sixteen-year-old girl from Barbados, moves to Salem in 1692. Kit is a free, white young woman who was raised by a loving grandfather and encouraged to read history, poetry, and plays. Kit is a misfit in the Puritan household of her aunt and stern-faced uncle. She meets the lonely, bent figure Quaker Hannah, also from Barbados, at the meadows near Blackbird Pond. Through Kit's spirited actions, she causes the townspeople to believe that her friend, Hannah, is the cause when sickness breaks out in the town. Kit risks her life to warn Hannah, and both escape before Hannah's cottage is burned by angry townsmen. Kit is arrested for witchcraft, and only with the assistance of her friends and relatives does she become acquitted of the charges.

Discussion and Beyond: Needing the Assistance of Relatives

With the students, discuss the changes in Kit's family arrangement, and contrast her life with her loving grandfather to her life with her stern uncle. Discuss the actions of Kit's aunt and uncle, and ask the older students to describe the changes each family member would have to undergo to become a more positive individual.

Target Activity: Changing the Characters in the Family

Building upon the above discussion, ask the students to rewrite a brief scene in the book that is full of family conflicts and misunderstandings by changing each character's negative responses to positive responses. When rewriting the scene, have students show how the family could have dealt with their concerns in a more loving and constructive way.

Yagawa, Sumiko (1981). *The Crane Wife.* **Illustrated by Suekichi Akabas. New York: Morrow.**

Heritage: Japanese

Family Context:

✦ **family conflict**

✦ **family support**

Genre: folk literature

Grades: 4–5

In this traditional Japanese tale about a husband's failure to heed the wife's good advice, a poor peasant man goes out into the winter snow and sees a crane that is wounded by an arrow and dragging its wing. The man removes the arrow from the crane and cares for the wound. Later that night, a beautiful woman appears at his door and asks to be his wife. The man agrees, and the woman, now his wife, offers to weave cloth to help buy food for them. Each time she weaves cloth, however, she warns her husband never to look in upon her. One day the husband becomes curious and looks in upon his wife's weaving. He sees a crane—not his wife—plucking her feathers to make the beautiful fabric. Once seen, the crane will not stay with the husband as a human wife, and she flies away.

Discussion and Beyond: Heed Good Advice in a Family

With the students, discuss the theme of heeding a wife's advice. Discuss other stories in which the advice of someone in the family is not heeded. From each story, write the advice and what happened when someone did not follow the advice on a chart for class reference.

Target Activity: Not Following the Good Advice of a Family Member

Ask the students to write a paragraph about a time when a family member gave them good advice and they did not follow it. What happened? How did it cause conflict in the family? Have them describe the consequences and what they learned from the experience. Have students share their writing with the class.

Namioka, Lensey (1992). *Yang the Youngest and His Terrible Ear.* **New York: Little, Brown.**

Heritage: Chinese

Family Context:

✦ family conflict

✦ diverse families

Genre: contemporary realistic fiction

Grades: 4–6

This story explores cultural and individual differences, and the problems a newcomer faces in a new environment. A recent immigrant to America from China, nine-year-old Yang Yingtao is tone deaf, and he is supposed to play in the family's string quartet. His father is a violinist in the Seattle Symphony, and Yang's performance will attest to his father's skill as a music teacher and bring honor to the family. Also, his father needs to teach more music students, to increase the family's income.

Discussion and Beyond: Family Expectations that Cause Conflict

With the students, discuss Yang's friendship with curly-haired Matthew. Discuss their contrary situations:

- Matthew's family wants him to practice baseball, but Matthew wants to play the violin.

- Yang's family wants him to excel at playing the violin, but he discovers that he has a natural affinity for baseball.

Ask students to discuss family expectations and why everyone needs to recognize this important part of family life of people and their abilities.

Target Activity: When Ambitions Cause Conflict

Discuss the universality of how one feels when faced with dreams or ambitions that run counter to the expectations of one's family members. Ask students to write an essay expressing a desire of theirs that may be different from the expectations that family members hold for them. Have them include:

1. What it is they want to do.

2. Their family's objection.

3. How they might resolve the conflict within their family.

Hooks, William H. (1990). *The Ballad of Belle Dorcas.* **Illustrated by Brian Pinkney. New York: Knopf.**

Heritage: African American

Family Context:

✦ family conflict

✦ mother-daughter relationship

Genre: folk literature

Grades: 4–6

This tale from the Gullah people tells of brave Belle Dorcas, a "free issue" person—the child of a slave master and a slave woman. Though free issues are free and generally marry other free issues, to take advantage of the relative freedom they are allowed, Belle Dorcas loves Joshua, a slave, and no one else will do. Pressured by her mother to marry one of the free issue young men, Belle goes on a hunger strike to let her mother know that she would sooner starve than marry someone other than Joshua. Her mother soon relents and allows Belle to marry Joshua, and they happily move to the slave quarters. When their old master dies, a new master, who cares only for money, decides to sell his strongest slave, Joshua. Belle runs to Granny Lizard, known for her magical spells, to get help for Joshua. Granny Lizard asks Belle, "Can you give up Joshua to keep him?" Without thinking, Belle answers "Yes" to the strange question. She is given a "conger" bag, a bag of magical herbs, to place around Joshua's neck. The night before Joshua is to be sold, Belle secretly slips the conger bag around Joshua's neck, and he turns into a cedar tree.

Discussion and Beyond: Disagreeing with a Parent

Ask students if they have ever had a strong disagreement with a parent about something that they wanted or did not want to do. What was the disagreement about? Did they understand their parent's point of view? Did their parent understand their point of view? How was the disagreement resolved? Ask students to imagine that many years have passed, they are a parent who has a child, and they are having a similar disagreement with their child. What is their point of view toward the child about this issue?

Target Activity: What This Hardship Did to the Family

Have students recount the hardships that slaves had to endure, as portrayed in this story. Ask them to imagine they are Belle, happily married to Joshua, and then the greedy master decides to sell him. Ask students to write a persuasive letter to the master, trying to convince him to allow Joshua to stay with his wife.

FAMILY PROBLEM SOLVING

Morrow, Barbara (1990). *Help for Mr. Peale.* Illustrated by the author. New York: Macmillan.

Heritage: European

Family Context:

✦ family problem solving

✦ family support

✦ father-son relationship

Genre: historical fiction

Grades: 4–6

In the late 1700s in Philadelphia, Mr. Charles Wilson Peale and his family are moving. They have artifacts of natural history to contribute to a new museum home, the first American natural-history museum in the area. Faced with the problem of how to transport such unusual things as exotic plants, large prehistoric bones, and stuffed animals, Peale's son, Ruben, organizes the children in the neighborhood to form a parade—its members carry the items to their new home, six blocks away.

Discussion and Beyond: Faced with a Family Problem

Ask the students to meet with partners to discuss a time when a family member was faced with a problem about how to do something, solve something, or respond to something in a particular way. Have partnerships organize a response to the problem. Ask the students to relate their experience to what goes on in the classroom every day by discussing a time when a class member was faced with a problem. Have them discuss how they could have organized a positive response to the problem. What could they have done to help? What will they do in the future if someone in the "classroom family" has a problem?

Target Activity: Family Problem Handbook

Ask students to think of a practical problem that their family was faced with recently. How did they solve the problem? Could other members of other families benefit from such problem solving? Encourage students to describe the family experience in writing, using the format:

Family problem: _____

Solution: _____

Other ways the problem could be solved: _____
_____

Incorporate all the problem-solving ideas into a class book titled "Family Problem Handbook."

Hall, Lynn (1981). *Danza.* **New York: Scribner's.**

Heritage: Puerto Rican

Family Context:

✦ family problem solving

✦ family heritage

✦ intergenerational relationship

Genre: contemporary realistic fiction

Grades: 6–8

Paulo Comacho wants to be as competent a horseman as his grandfather. He is proud of the Paso Fino horses on the ranch—his favorite is the stallion, Danza, whom he has raised from birth. When Danza needs care, Paulo travels to the United States and cares for the horse during its recovery. In America, Paulo comes to a better understanding of himself, his grandfather, and his love for Puerto Rico.

Discussion and Beyond:
Pride in My Family

Ask students if they have a close or extended family member of whom they are particularly proud, perhaps because they would like to be just like this person. Invite students to share the name of this person, their relationship, why this person makes them feel proud, and how this person has helped them solve problems and resolve conflicts.

Target Activity:
Problem Solving in Paulo's Family

After hearing the story and learning about Paulo and his family, ask the students to use chalk to convert the floor of the classroom into an architectural blueprint stage for the setting of the story. Have students mark such locations as Puerto Rico, Florida, New Mexico, and Arizona. When the stage is complete, ask some students to play the roles of people in the story, focusing on how problems were solved in the story. Have the rest of the class watch the role play and take notes about how the roles are performed. After the role play, have the students who watched suggest alternative solutions to the problems.

Hamilton, Virginia (1974). *M. C. Higgins, the Great.* **New York: Macmillan.**

Heritage: African American

Family Context:

✦ family problem solving

Genre: contemporary realistic fiction

Grades: 7+

Living on Sarah Mountain near the Ohio River, M. C. sees an enormous spoil heap, left by stripminers, that is oozing slowly down the hill toward his family's house. This place has been home to his family since 1854, when his great-grandmother Sarah, a runaway slave, found refuge here. When his father refuses to accept the danger of the landslide, M. C. realizes that he must save the family. To divert the slide, M. C. builds a wall of earth, reinforced with branches, old automobile fenders, and a gravestone. The story concentrates on M. C.'s interactions with his family: Ben Killburn, the child of a family shunned by the neighbors; Luhretta Outlaw, a strange girl; and James K. Lewis, who travels through the hills and records folk songs on his tape recorder.

Discussion and Beyond: Acting to Save Your Family

With older students (grades 6+), discuss the concept of acting to save your family in times of adversity. M. C. acts to save his family. He builds a wall of earth, reinforced with branches, automobile fenders, and old Sarah's gravestone. M. C. proves himself "great" when he takes positive action to save his home from the spoil heap. Invite students to share a time when they, or another family member, took positive action to save their family.

Target Activity: Coming Together in Adversity

Sometimes when families experience difficult problems, they become stronger; other families are pushed apart from one another. M. C. Higgins's family became stronger in the end. Have students think of a time their family faced a crisis situation (e.g., financial, ill health, a death, a robbery, a natural disaster, etc.). Ask students to write a reflective paragraph about the event, explaining whether it brought them closer together or pushed them farther apart.

FAMILY CONCERNS

Manes, Stephen (1992). *Comedy High.* **New York: Scholastic.**

Heritage: European

Family Context:

✦ family concerns

✦ father-son relationship

Genre: contemporary realistic fiction

Grades: 6+

Ivan Zeller and his father move to Carmody, Nevada, a town that advertises itself as the "Future Entertainment Capital of the World." They find Carmody's water almost undrinkable, its smelly air almost unbreathable, and its desert heat and dryness almost unbearable. Even though Ivan's cousin, Gilda, keeps telling him how fantastic the town's new high school will be once it has been relocated into a renovated hotel/casino, only his newly acquired friendships and his sense of humor make the new town bearable.

Discussion and Beyond: Facing Strange Situations

Poll students as to how many of them have relocated from one town, state, or country to another. Ask them to share their initial reactions they had to the new place. Ask them to describe the effect the move had on each family member and on the family as a whole. What attitudes and behaviors on the part of all family members would be especially helpful in such a situation? How might Ivan's father have better smoothed the transition for his son? Why did he not help his son more?

Target Activity: Telling a Family Member About a New School

Discuss with students the exciting possibilities of attending a school such as this one in Carmody. The story ends just a few days after the new school opens, but more remains to be told about this innovative learning environment. Have students play the role of Ivan and write a long note to his father about the exciting and humorous things that happen to Ivan and his two new friends, the offbeat Greb and the "with-it" Caitlin, while they attend their classes at the "fabulous" new high school in the hotel/casino environment.

Franklin, Kristine (1995). *Eclipse.* **Cambridge, MA: Candlewick.**

Heritage: European

Family Context:

✦ family concerns

✦ family adversity

Genre: realistic fiction

Grades: 6-8

While trying to deal with the concerns of the average pre-adolescent girl, Trina must also cope with serious family problems: Her father has suffered a nervous breakdown, and her mother has become pregnant at the age of forty-eight. Trina is feeling severely frustrated with her rapidly changing life. Not only is her body changing and her school relationships becoming more complex, but her family life is coming unraveled. Trina realizes she must now become the strong one in the family.

Discussion and Beyond: "The Desiderata"

Write on the chalkboard the anonymously written, nondenominational prayer "The Desiderata":

> God grant me the serenity to accept the things I cannot change; courage to change the things I can; and wisdom to know the difference.

Discuss with students the meaning of this prayer. How would such a philosophy have helped Trina? How might it be helpful in students' lives?

Target Activity: Deciding What Can Be Changed

To follow up on the above discussion, make two columns on the chalkboard. Label one "Things I can change" and the other "Things I cannot change." Brainstorm with students what to list under each column. Ask students to write a two-paragraph essay delineating the things in their life that they would like to change but discriminating between those things that they can change and those things that they cannot change. Encourage students to read their essays aloud for further discussion.

Highwater, Jamake (1977). *Anpao: An American Indian Odyssey.* **Illustrated by Fritz Scholder. Philadelphia: Lippincott.**

Heritage: Native American

Family Context:

✦ **family concerns**

✦ **family support**

Genre: folk literature

Grades: 6–8

In this Blackfeet legend of Scarface, scarred Anpao (whose name means "Dawn") goes on a Ulysses-type quest to obtain the permission of the Sun to marry beautiful Ko-ko-mik-e-is. After befriending Morning Star (whose parents are the Sun and the Moon) on a journey through a terrible desert, Anpao saves Morning Star from monster birds. In return, the Sun removes the scars from Anpao and recognizes Anpao as the long-lost son of both the mighty Sun and an earth woman. On his journey home, Anpao meets Smallpox, who tells Anpao that sooner or later everyone will come to know Smallpox and that all the people he visits will die (a reflection on the Blackfeet's experience with the white man). Carrying beautiful gifts from the Sun, Moon, and Morning Star, Anpao returns to Ko-ko-mik-e-is, marries her, and they live happily in a village below a great water.

Discussion and Beyond: Marriage Expectations in Other Times and Cultures

Ask students if it is still common for young people to ask permission of their parents if they wish to get married. Ask students from other countries about their customs for marriage and gaining permission. Discuss marriage customs historically, in the United States and in other countries. Ask students to interview older members of their extended family, such as grandparents, great-aunts, and great-uncles, about past marriage customs and how marriage customs have changed. Encourage students to share what they learned with the class.

Target Activity: Comparing Parents in Folk Literature and Real Life

Discuss the events of Anpao's quest: his journey through the terrible desert, his victory over the monster birds, his rescue of Morning Star, and his homecoming and marriage to Ko-ko-mik-e-is. Record the events in sequence on the chalkboard, and ask the students to paint a mural recreating the sequenced events. Pair students together, and have each partnership contribute one image to the mural. Encourage students to consult the story as needed to obtain information for their drawings. After the mural is complete, have each partnership write a narrative to explain their event and place the narrative beneath their section of the mural, in sequence, for others to read.

Conly, Jane Leslie (1993). *Crazy Lady!* **New York: HarperCollins.**

Heritage: European

Family Context:

◆ family concerns

◆ family conflict

◆ single father

Genre: contemporary realistic fiction

Grades: 5–8

No one in his family notices that Vernon is failing academically, and Vernon is quietly desperate, unable to resolve his problems. He joins other boys who tease the alcoholic woman, Maxine, and her retarded son, Roland. When he stands up for her one day at the grocery store, she makes kind comments about his dead mother. In a moment of trust, Vernon tells Maxine about his troubles at school. Maxine introduces Vernon to a retired teacher, Miss Annie, who tutors him and asks as payment only that Vernon help Maxine and Roland.

Discussion and Beyond: Talking It Over

As a class, ask students how it feels to be excluded from the family in times of trouble. How does it feel to be accepted and loved? Ask why it is sometimes easier to talk about problems with people outside the family. Ask the students to recall the compassionate side of Vernon's character—the cruel side and the compassionate side. How did Vernon help Maxine and Roland repay Miss Annie?

Target Activity: Someone Outside the Family Can Be Like Family

Ask students to think of a time when it was difficult to talk about a problem with a family member and they turned to someone outside the family. Ask them to share this experience with a partner in the classroom. As a class, elicit from students what people outside a family can be like a family member (e.g., neighbor, community youth group leader, religious leader, teacher, school counselor, etc.).

George, Jean Craighead (1989). *Shark Beneath the Reef.* **New York: Harper & Row.**

Heritage: Hispanic

Family Context:

✦ family concerns

✦ family heritage

✦ family problem solving

✦ father-son relationship

Genre: contemporary realistic fiction

Grades: 5-6

Tomas Torres, a young Hispanic Indian, loves his life as a fisherman in the waters off the coast of Baja. Times are changing: Government interference threatens to destroy life as Tomas and his family have known it in the past. The change forces the family to make a decision about Tomas's life: Should he continue to fish and try to cling to the old, familiar way of life or go to school and work toward a new way? Tomas's emotional struggle is symbolized through a fight with a huge shark—in the end, Tomas finds a compromise.

Discussion and Beyond: All Families Face Stress

One way for a student to experience what it is like to cope with stress successfully is to read stories about children from other cultures who are the same age as the reader and who have coped with stress by being resilient. Discuss this with students, and ask them to suggest books that could be assembled into a classroom reference display about coping with stress.

Target Activity: Family Problem Solving in Two Cultures

Ask the students to discuss similarities and differences between problem solving in their lives in America and problem solving as portrayed in the story. Write the comparisons on the chalkboard, and ask students to suggest how the comparisons can be categorized in a comparison chart. Invite students to discuss the necessity of problem solving as a family in every culture.

HOMELESSNESS

Wolf, Bernard (1995). *Homeless.* **Photographs by the author. New York: Orchard Press.**

Heritage: European

Family Context:

✦ homelessness

Genre: nonfiction

Grades: 4–8

The topic of homelessness is sensitively treated in this photo essay that shows how a family center offers help to homeless families. The book follows a child and his family as center workers assist them in finding temporary housing, food, schools, employment options, and other services. The color photographs are vivid portrayals a family faced with a difficult challenge of finding the strength to stay together and seeking the help they need.

Discussion and Beyond: Not Blaming the Victim

Ask students if they have ever had a problem that was so difficult to solve that they thought they needed help from an adult. Have them discuss this situation with a trusted classmate. Ask students if they have ever seen adults on the street with a sign saying that they are "homeless" and that they "will work for food." What do they think when they see these people? How do the adults around them react to this situation? Ask students if they have revised their thinking about homelessness after reading this book, and if there might have been a time in the lives of most adults when they, in one way or another, needed a helping hand.

Target Activity: An Essay of Revision

The realism of this nonfiction book strikes a chord in many young readers. Have them share new insights by writing a two-paragraph essay revealing any change in their feelings toward the homeless. The first paragraph might begin, "Before reading this book I thought homeless people _____." The second paragraph might begin, "After reading this book I feel differently about the homeless in these ways."

Nixon, Joan Lowery (1988). *A Family Apart.* **New York: Bantam.**

Heritage: European

Family Context:

✦ homelessness

✦ single mother

Genre: historical fiction

Grades: 4–6

Thousands of homeless children wandered the streets of New York City in the early 1800s. In 1856, Mrs. Kelly places her six children in Reverend Brace's hands because she can no longer support or care for them. The Kelly children board the Orphan Train for St. Joseph, Missouri. They are placed in different homes. The oldest child, thirteen-year-old Frances Mary, and the youngest child are placed in a home together. In her new family, Frances Mary becomes part of the Underground Railroad.

Discussion and Beyond: A Need for Support and Care

Pair students together to discuss situations when someone needed support or care. What social agencies could have helped the person in need? Ask the students to share how they helped someone who needed care or support. Discuss situations when a class member needed support or care. What could they have done to help? What will they do in the future if someone in their "classroom family" needs support or care?

Target Activity: Family Services

Have students do community research to learn all they can about how children are cared for and placed in homes when their biological parents have died or are unable to care for them. Provide the names and telephone numbers of agencies in the community for students to contact. Ask students to share with the class the information they have assembled. Discuss the differences and similarities between how orphaned children are cared for today and what happened to the Kelly children when they were in need of a family.

Nixon, Joan Lowery (1990). *In the Face of Danger.* **New York: Bantam.**

Heritage: European

Family Context:

+ homelessness
+ family concerns

Genre: historical fiction

Grades: 4–6

Twelve-year-old Megan Kelly wrongly believes that it is her fault that her mother was forced to send the children on the Orphan Train. At her new home, Megan continues to believe that she brings bad luck and causes the natural disasters and some of the political unrest of the times. She breaks her streak of bad luck, however, when she saves her new mother and friends and holds an accused murderer captive.

Discussion and Beyond: Getting the Wrong Idea

Ask the students to meet in partnerships to discuss times they know of when they "got the wrong idea" about something, just as Megan Kelly did. Was there ever a time when they believed something that happened was their fault? Ask them to explain how they finally realized that they had gotten the wrong idea. Ask the students to relate their experience to what happens in the classroom every day: Have them discuss a time when they got the wrong idea about a member of the class or about something that happened in the classroom. Have them discuss how they could have cleared up the matter and gotten the right idea.

Target Activity: Facing Difficult Situations

Megan Kelly attributes much of what has happened in her life to either good luck or bad luck. Have students write about a recent positive or negative experience that they have had with their families. Ask them to analyze the experience for its causes, describing how it might seem to be related to luck but is actually related more to hard work, or other causes that have a logical explanation.

O'Dell, Scott (1960). *Island of the Blue Dolphins.* **Boston: Houghton Mifflin.**

Heritage: Native American

Family Context:

◆ **homelessness**

◆ **death in the family**

◆ **sibling relationship**

Genre: historical fiction

Grades: 5–7

This book is based on a true story: Off the California coast (near present-day Los Angeles) on the island of San Nicolas, twelve-year-old Karana survived alone for eighteen years in the 1800s. In 1853, a ship's crew took her to the California mainland. Karana and her six-year-old brother, Ramo, were left behind when their people were being removed by ship from their homes. During Karen's struggles for survival on the island after her brother Ramo is killed by wild dogs, she makes a fenced-in house and a cave dwelling. Karana is a strong female with positive character traits: She is brave, competent, intelligent, and independent. Her story is not only a story of survival in the face of disaster but also a story of a human's need to love and be loved.

Discussion and Beyond: Understanding What It Is Like Without a Family

With students, discuss the following questions:

1. What is it like to be lonely and without a family? Describe Karana's need to love and be loved by others.

2. Karana learned that people were islands without a family, yet secure unto themselves and part of humanity where all could "transgress our limits in reverence for all life." How did she come to this realization?

3. In what ways did Karana show her reverence for all life? In what way did she transgress her limits?

Target Activity: Surviving Alone

Ask students to think of a nearby wilderness area, nature area, bike trail, jogging path, or other isolated spot and imagine that they somehow became lost there and had to live by themselves for a few years. Have them write a series of journal entries describing what they did for food, shelter, entertainment, and so on, especially focusing on newfound appreciations that might emerge for family members. Encourage students to read one entry to the class.

George, Jean Craighead (1972). *Julie of the Wolves.* **New York: Harper & Row.**

Heritage: Native American

Family Context:
+ homelessness
+ family heritage
+ family traditions

Genre: contemporary realistic fiction

Grades: 6–8

Thirteen-year-old Julie Miyax, an Eskimo girl, leaves Daniel, the husband her father selected for her. She proceeds across the tundra toward Point Hope, where she plans to leave for San Francisco to find a California pen pal, Amy. Lost, Julie survives only because of her knowledge of Eskimo lore (setting her course by migrating birds and the North Star) and her friendship with Amaroq, the leader of a wolf pack. This story portrays the coming together of two cultures: Julie lives as the traditional Eskimo did, but she also returns to her father, Kapugen, and accepts the fact that he has abandoned his former way of life, married a white woman (a gussak) from the lower states, and hunts from a plane for sport rather than for food.

Discussion and Beyond: Changes in a Family's Life

Ask the students to imagine that they are a friend of Julie's and Julie tells them what is happening in her life. Julie is about to leave her husband, a man who has been selected by her father. Julie is unhappy because she has learned that her father has married a white woman. She knows, too, that he has changed his former way of life and now hunts for sport rather than just for food. How would the students help Julie? What would they say to her?

Target Activity: Living off the Land

Ask students to consider three qualities that a person would need to leave their traditional life and begin to depend on no one but themselves for survival. Did Julie display these qualities? How? Invite students to write a three-paragraph essay delineating how Julie displayed the three qualities, one in each paragraph, and providing evidence through direct quotations from the story.

Hamilton, Virginia (1971). *The Planet of Junior Brown.* **New York: Macmillan.**

Heritage: African American

Family Context:
+ homelessness
+ family concerns
+ mother-son relationship

Genre: contemporary realistic fiction

Grades: 6–10

In the eighth grade, Junior Brown is a talented pianist who weighs more than 250 pounds. His friend, big Buddy Clark, is brilliant in science and math, works part-time at a newsstand, and leads a group of homeless boys who live on a "planet" of their own in the basement of an abandoned house. Junior and Buddy spend their time with a janitor, Mr. Poole, a former math and astronomy teacher, in his basement room behind a false wall in the broom closet. Frustration after frustration affects Junior as he slips away from reality.

Discussion and Beyond:
Those Who Help Others as Family

Ask students to consider what they would have done to help the boys if they had been with them when:

1. The group of homeless boys visit their "planet" in the basement of an abandoned house.

2. Neither of the boys goes to classes at school for two and one-half months.

Target Activity:
One Week as a Homeless Person

Have students plan and execute the painting of a mural depicting the life of a homeless person, as portrayed in this story as well as in other sources. Have students write stories, based on the mural, about the adventures of children who have no homes, focusing on their family lives, problems at school, and experiences in their communities during a typical week. Discuss what children might do to help other children who are less fortunate than themselves.

FAMILY SUPPORT

Hudson, Jan (1989). *Sweetgrass.* **New York: Philomel.**

Heritage: Native American

Family Context:

✦ family support

✦ illness in the family

✦ family responsibilities

Genre: historical fiction

Grades: 4–6

Sweetgrass, a young Blackfoot girl, faces a life-threatening struggle against smallpox, the white man's disease, in 1837. Her story is based on written records that document the spread of the disease and the harsh winter of 1837–38 for her people. As she approaches womanhood, Sweetgrass fulfills her obligations to her family and others but does not allow tribal omens to control her life. She selects some of her people's omens to help her family members against the disease. Becoming a woman, she feels "mightier than a brave" and believes that she can see the future like she sees the summer berries in her hands. She is determined to make her life what she wants it to be. A bibliography for further reading is included.

Discussion and Beyond: A Life-or-Death Struggle

Ask students if anyone in their immediate or extended family has ever endured a life-or-death struggle against illness or as the result of an accident. Invite students to share their story about the struggle. How did family members offer support? How did family members grow closer together—or end up farther apart—as a result of the struggle?

Target Activity: Living Through a Natural Catastrophe

Brainstorm some natural catastrophes that have occurred in the last forty or fifty years in your area, such as floods, droughts, forest fires, blizzards, earthquakes, hurricanes, and tornadoes. Ask students if they can remember any family stories about living through such catastrophes that are in any way reminiscent of Sweetgrass's ordeal. Have students write a fictitious story, or one based upon their family's recollections, about a family living through a natural catastrophe.

Love, D. Anne (1995). *Bess's Log Cabin Quilt.* **New York: Holiday House.**

Heritage: European

Family Context:

✦ family support

✦ family crisis

✦ absent father

Genre: historical fiction

Grades: 4–6

This story movingly portrays a young girl's love for her family and her determination to achieve her goals. The fictional account concerns the young girl and her mother, who live in a cabin in Oregon while the father works on the Oregon Trail guiding the settlers west. When the mother becomes ill with swamp fever, a stranger comes by to tell them that he will take their farm if they do not pay him the money the father borrowed. To save their home, Bess hurries to finish her log cabin quilt so she can enter a contest that offers a cash prize—if she wins, she can repay the debt.

Discussion and Beyond: Qualities That Make a family

Discuss with students the qualities that make a family as opposed to, simply, a group of people who live together. What qualities did Bess and her family display? What qualities have members of their family displayed that show the commitment they have for one another?

Target Activity: Pitching In to Help the Family

Ask students to close their eyes while you lead them in a guided-imagery activity about a family crisis in which they are in danger of losing their home (this imagery can be taken directly from a scene in the story, *Bess's Log Cabin Quilt*). Ask students to consider what they might be able to do to assist their family with such a hardship. Have students brainstorm "hidden" talents they have—such as the ability to mow lawns, babysit, shovel snow, or rake leaves—that might be exploited for cash. This activity can empower students by helping them feel more in control of their lives and by helping them realize that they do not need to be powerless victims when misfortune confronts them.

Yep, Laurence (1984). *The Serpent People.* **New York: Harper & Row.**

Heritage: Chinese

Family Context:

◆ family support

◆ family adversity

◆ two-parent family

Genre: historical fiction

Grades: 6+

The 1900s were a time of ongoing battles in China. China's people fought with those who supported Manchu and British dominance in the land. In this turmoil, a young girl finds the strength to protect her family, and she finds strength in their support of her. Yep's vivid descriptions of Chinese culture at that time, set against a backdrop of national strife, offer a rare glimpse into the infrastructure of family life in China.

Discussion and Beyond: Cultural Stereotypes About Families Can Be Incorrect

Discuss some of the many incorrect stereotypes about people and families from different cultures. List the students' suggestions on the chalkboard. Have students speculate about how these stereotypes might have originated. Discuss the stereotypes considering changes that may be taking place today.

Target Activity: Experiences of Supportive Families

Divide the class into four groups, and engage each group in the project of finding evidence (photographs, interview notes, articles) about traditions, beliefs, and experiences from different cultures. Each student should be responsible for conducting part of the research. Ask students to take particular notice of how families in the diverse cultures support one another. Meet with each group to discuss the traditions, beliefs, experiences, and support mechanisms. Have each group transform their research into a presentation for the class (e.g., written report, mural, set of posters, etc.).

Herrera, Juan Felipe (1996). *Calling the Doves/El Canto de las Palomas.* **Illustrated by Elly Simmons. Chicago: Children's Book Press.**

Heritage: Hispanic

Family Context:

◆ **family support**

◆ **family traditions**

Genre: autobiography

Grades: 4–6

In Spanish and English, Herrera recounts his early life, spent growing up in a migrant farm-working family. Images of night skies, bright mornings, and valley landscapes are richly illustrated in words and pictures. Stories full of poetry and tradition told by loving parents provide the constancy and foundation from which the narrator looks back and remembers all he has learned from his wonderful family.

Discussion and Beyond: The Beauty of Family Memories

This book will often incite the reader to share memories of places and sensations experienced in family life. Read aloud some of the descriptive phrases in the book while students close their eyes. As a class, revisit students' favorite illustrations. What do these images remind them of? What places do they remember fondly and long to return to?

Target Activity: Painting a Memory

Provide students with watercolor paints, white construction paper, and paintbrushes. Ask them to select their favorite description from the book as inspiration, or encourage them to paint a place or image they remember from their family life. Invite students to share their painting and what it represents to them.

Clark, Ann Nolan (1978). *To Stand Against the Wind.* **New York: Viking.**

Heritage: Vietnamese

Family Context:

✦ family support

✦ mother-daughter relationship

Genre: contemporary realistic fiction

Grades: 5+

Preparing for their traditional Day of the Ancestors—to honor and remember those who have died—Elm, now the head of his household, records the family's history and tells them about a country they may never know. In this emotional story told by eleven-year-old Elm, a refugee now living in America, the boy helps his grandmother, older sister, and uncle prepare for the holiday. He remembers the beautiful Vietnam country along the Mekong River delta that was his family's home for centuries. He recalls the bombing of his village and the death of many of his family members, especially his father. He remembers his village, with its buildings burning and the nearby dikes destroyed. To journey to America, Elm and his remaining family are sponsored by a church group.

Discussion and Beyond: Children in All Families Can "Stand Against the Wind"

With students, discuss what Elm remembers about his life in Vietnam: his father, who loved the land, and the American reporter who often visited them to learn more about the people in the village. As Elm remembers more about the war, he recalls some of the members of his family going off to fight,

the fall of Saigon, and the day when his village was bombed. After this, he finds his mother, father, and other family members dead. With students, discuss Elm's journey to America with the remaining members of his family, which was sponsored by a church group. How did these strangers help this family "stand against the wind"?

Target Activity: A Vietnamese Family's History

Ask students to select descriptive words, pictures, and phrases from the book to better understand the culture and lifestyle of this family. Have students suggest categories (e.g., food, clothing, shelter, customs, etc.) that can be used to compare their lives with the lives of family members in this story. If appropriate, ask students to investigate the yellow pages of the local telephone directory to note the different groups of people, particularly Vietnamese, who live in their area. Have students ask questions about the former lives of families from Vietnam who live in their area. Invite a Vietnamese immigrant to speak to your class and answer some of the students' questions.

FAMILY CRISIS

Morrison, L. (1937). *The Last Queen of Egypt.* **Illustrated by F. Geritz and W. Brunton. New York: Lippincott.**

Heritage: Middle Eastern/Egypt

Family Context:

◆ family crisis

◆ death in the family

◆ two-parent family

Genre: historical fiction

Grades: 4–6

About 1580 B.C., the Pharaoh of Egypt; Nefertiti, his queen; and their six little daughters met in the royal nurseries of Akhenaten with the Great Royal Mother. She decides that three of the little girls should be betrothed at once to guarantee the succession. Tutankhaten, a soldier, is chosen for Ankesenpaten, who is pleased with the choice because he has shown bravery equal to her own. Later, the two inherit the throne as Tutankhamon and Ankhsenamon. Instead of a long and happy reign, the young king dies by poisoning, and the queen must choose marriage to the traitorous Ay or death.

Discussion and Beyond: The Importance of Sons in Other Cultures

Discuss the fact that in ancient Egypt, having six female offspring was considered a curse, and much pressure was put upon females to give birth to sons. Discuss how this is still true in some countries today, such as China, where sons provide parents with their "social security." Ask students to share how parents in this country feel about giving birth to daughters versus sons.

Target Activity: Comparing Daughters

Engage students, working in small groups, to consider the differences between the lives of the daughters of the Pharaoh in ancient Egypt and the life of the daughter of a president of the United States. Encourage them to research marriage arrangements for young people and other customs in the ancient Egyptian culture and compare the arrangements with those in America today. Why do these ancient customs differ from current American customs? Do any of these ancient customs prevail in Egypt today? Why?

Frank, Anne (1952). *Anne Frank: The Diary of a Young Girl.* **New York: Doubleday.**

Heritage: European

Family Context:

◆ family crisis

◆ family conflict

◆ family support

Genre: autobiography

Grades: 6+

This autobiography is an account of the changes in the lives of eight people. They hid for two years in a secret annex of an office building in Amsterdam. Over the two years, Anne records her gradual change from a little girl to a young woman. She vents to her diary about her volatile relationships with her parents, her sister, and the others hiding in the annex, vividly describing how nerves are frayed with the limited space and resources. The eight people were finally found and imprisoned by the Nazis. After the war, the diary was found by Anne's father, the only one of the eight to survive.

Discussion and Beyond:
A Family in Crisis

Discuss how this extraordinary crisis brought out the best and the worst in family members. Ask students if there was anything exceptional about Anne Frank's family, or if any family would have fared about the same under the same circumstances.

Target Activity:
Diary of Family Life

Have students keep a diary of their family life for one week, focusing on their interactions with each member of their immediate and extended families. Using dialogue, ask them to write down conversations, discussions, and even disputes. Upon reviewing the week's diary, ask them to share in small groups what they learned from tracking the interactions in their family.

Blume, Judy (1981). *Tiger Eyes.* **New York: Dell.**

Heritage: European

Family Context:

✦ family crisis

✦ death of a family member

✦ single mother

Genre: contemporary realistic fiction

Grades: 5–8

Dancy Wexler's father has just been shot to death in a 7-Eleven store. Dancy cannot believe that something this tragic could happen to her. Her mother is close to a nervous breakdown, and her younger brother is too young to realize what is happening. The family moves to New Mexico to stay with relatives until they can adjust to their new, smaller family. Feeling alone and confused, Dancy finds a private place where she can go and be alone—the Los Alamos Canyon. There she meets a young boy about her age named Wolf, who understands how angry she is feeling. He has also faced profound losses in his life; he encourages Dancy to continue to pursue life as he has.

Discussion and Beyond:
Sharing Feelings

Have students reflect upon someone other than members of their family to whom they might go when they have problems. Why did they select this person? What can they share with this person that they cannot share with family members? How is their relationship with this person helpful?

Target Activity: Appreciation Circle

Gather students in a circle. Ask them to think about a person in their life who helps them when they have problems. Have students, in turn, share with others the appreciation they feel for this person, using the phrase: "I appreciate _____ because _____ ."
Students should feel free to "pass" if they cannot think of someone immediately.

de Jenkins, Lyll Becerra (1988). *The Honorable Prison.* **New York: Lodestar Books/E. P. Dutton.**

Heritage: South American

Family Context:
◆ family crisis
◆ absent father
◆ family illness
◆ family support

Genre: historical fiction

Grades: 7–8

In South America in the mid-1950s, the Maldonado family members become political prisoners. When Marta's father, a journalist, criticizes the dictator of the country, Marta's family is arrested and confined to a bare hut. Marta, her parents, and her young brother, Ricardo, cope with fear of execution, hunger, isolations, and an awareness that Mr. Maldonado is dying of a lung ailment. There are some similarities to Anne Frank's *The Diary of a Young Girl* (see p. 121).

Discussion and Beyond: Does Adversity Bring a Family Closer?

Ask students from families who have recently encountered natural disasters such as floods, tornadoes, or earthquakes to share, in small groups, their impressions of how this adversity affected their family and family members' relationships to one another.

Target Activity: Marta's or Ricardo's Journal

Taking the role of either Marta or Ricardo, have students create a week of journal entries as the two children might have written them while they and their family were coping with the horrific conditions in their small hut. Review the importance of dialogue to vivid, appealing writing, and encourage students to incorporate the conversations of family members as they might have occurred under these adverse conditions. If desired, have students read aloud the dialogues in small groups.

ALCOHOL AND DRUG ABUSE

Bennett, Paul (1987). *Follow the River.* **New York: Orchard Books/Watts.**

Heritage: European

Family Context:

✦ alcoholism

✦ family diversity

✦ mother-son relationship

Genre: historical fiction

Grades: 6+

In the 1930s in the town of Gnadenhutten, Harry Lighthorse Lee, one of six sons, is ashamed to take his mother's laundry work back to the Suttons because he does not want Nancy Sutton, the banker's daughter, to know his mother does laundry. A good student, Lighthorse applies to the college that Nancy plans to attend. Nancy and Lighthorse fall in love and resolve their differences as they struggle through the days of the Great Depression, which are made more difficult by the alcoholism of Nancy's mother.

Discussion and Beyond: Empathizing with Family Members

Discuss how it is always helpful to concentrate on the positive traits that family members have, even when family members are experiencing problems.

Ask each student to name one thing that a member of their family can do well. Encourage a variety of different responses, and list them on the chalkboard. Discuss the similarities and differences among these talents.

Target Activity: Getting Help

Have students, working in small groups, discuss the options Nancy might have explored when she realized that her mother was an alcoholic, such as share her concerns with a trusted adult, or call a local agency that deals with the problem of alcoholism. Invite students to select a spokesperson for the group and share the results of their discussion with the rest of the class. Optionally, have students explore this topic further and create a small handbook that offers advice to children whose significant other is affected by alcoholism.

Bauer, G. (1976). *Shelter from the Wind.* **New York: Seabury Press.**

Heritage: European

Family Context:

✦ alcoholism

✦ family adversity

✦ intergenerational relationship

✦ stepfamilies

Genre: contemporary realistic fiction

Grades: 5–8

In running away to search for the alcoholic mother who has deserted her, twelve-year-old Stacy comes to terms with pain as a requisite of life. Her adventure leads not to her mother, but to Old Ella, an elderly women who also has known desertion. Stacy thinks that she is seeking her real mother because she hates her now-pregnant step-mother. Old Ella teaches her otherwise. Fast-paced events enable Stacy to expand her capacities. The key incident concerns the mercy-killing of a new-born puppy, at whose birth Stacy is present. In performing the act, Stacy, who has previously been unable to cry, finally unleashes all the grief she has been keeping inside.

Discussion and Beyond: Running Away from Family Problems

Ask students if they have ever run away or thought about running away from their families. Invite them to share these experiences in small groups.

Brainstorm, with the use of an overhead transparency or chalkboard, alternative solutions (e.g., talking to a trusted adult friend, confronting the family member, changing their behavior, etc.) if students are experiencing problems with a family member. Encourage students to role play some of these situations and alternative solutions.

Target Activity: Advice from Caring Adults

Sometimes caring adults in the life of a child can help them cope with events in their life, as Old Ella helped Stacy. Ask students if they have such a person in their lives. Have them write a letter to this person, thanking them for specific times they have provided love, support, and insight into their family life. Invite students to send the letter to the person if desired (these letters need not be shared, even with the teacher).

Zindel, Paul (1983). *Pardon Me, You're Stepping on My Eyeball.* New York: Harper & Row.

Heritage: European

Family Context:

✦ alcoholism

✦ absent father

✦ death in the family

✦ mother-son relationship

Genre: contemporary realistic fiction

Grades: 5–8

This novel is a poignant commentary on misfit teenagers contrasted with a laugh-a-page format. Marsh lives with his mother, an abusive alcoholic, and pretends that his father is still alive. Marsh meets a girl named Edna, whose ego-destroying parents inflict another kind of abuse. Supporting each other through their difficulties with open communication, Marsh is eventually able to revisit his father, symbolically, and say good-bye to him at which point he no longer denies his father's death to himself or others. The true-to-life dialogue of teenagers strengthens the meaning of the story.

Discussion and Beyond: Pretending Things Are Different

Ask students why Marsh pretended his father was still alive and glorified his memory. Is this behavior deceptive? Why? Ask students if they have ever wished that their family conformed more closely to some idealized model. What is that idealized model? Discuss whether it is helpful to know that every family has its problems and concerns.

Target Activity: Friends Support Family Life

Ask students if they have ever confided in a close friend in a way that they would not have to their family members. Explain that this is perfectly normal. Ask students to write a paragraph about something a family member did that upset them, and then encourage students to reconstruct a dialogue that they had with a friend about the incident. Have them close the paragraph by revealing how they felt after sharing their problem with the friend.

DEATH IN THE FAMILY

Whelan, Gloria (1992). *A Time to Keep Silent*. **Grand Rapids, MI: Wm. B. Eerdmans.**

Heritage: European

Family Context:

◆ death in the family

◆ family conflicts

◆ father-daughter relationship

Genre: contemporary realistic fiction

Grades: 5–8

Thirteen-year-old Clair Lothrop's family is falling apart. Her mother has died, and her father spends his evenings shut in his study. In a desperate attempt to get her father's attention, Clair stops talking. Clair's silence gets her father's attention, but not in the way she had hoped. He resigns from his position as pastor of a large metropolitan church to begin a mission in the remote woods of northern Michigan, taking Clair with him. Clair is furious about having to move, but everything changes when Clair discovers a wonderful new friend her own age, Dorrie, who lives alone in the woods. Through this surprising friendship, Clair finds strength and courage she did not know she had.

Discussion and Beyond: A Time to Keep Silent—A Time to Talk

With the students, discuss how it is sometimes helpful to talk about grief that they are experiencing and that by keeping it bottled up they can often feel worse. Invite students to share, in small groups, a time when someone dear to them, even a beloved pet, died. Encourage them to share who they spoke to about the event and how they felt after sharing.

Target Activity: A Letter of Comfort

Allow students to select a partner with whom they feel comfortable. Have partnerships discuss their ideas, religious or otherwise, about death and what might happen when a person or an animal dies. If they have had an experience in this regard, ask them to share who or what made them feel comforted about the death and what they learned that they could share with others their age. Using the ideas from their discussion, have students write a letter of comfort to Clair that might have helped her deal more easily with the death of her mother.

Rappaport, Doreen (1995). *The New King*. **Illustrated by Emily Arnold McCully. New York: Dial.**

Heritage: Asian

Family Context:

◆ death in the family

Genre: historical fiction

Grades: 4–6

A young Malagasy prince refuses to believe that his father's death is final. With his newfound power, he commands the Royal Magician, Royal Doctor, and High Counselor to bring his father back to life. Of course, they cannot. He runs to the Wise Woman, who explains death in terms he can understand. She reassures him that the former king will live forever as part of the young king's life through the lessons passed from father to son. Vivid watercolors portray life in Madagascar during the nineteenth century.

Discussion and Beyond:
Leaving a Legacy

Ask students to consider how the Wise Woman's advice helped the new king accept his father's death. Discuss how every person leaves behind a legacy, whether good or bad. Ask students to brainstorm positive lessons they have learned from observing the significant adults in their lives. What lessons do they hope to pass on to their children?

Target Activity:
Legacy from a Loved One

Ask students to write an essay about one or more important lessons they have learned from a parent or caretaker that they will pass on to successive generations. Have students revise their essays using peer editors. Have students mount the final drafts on construction paper and create colorful borders. Encourage them to present the essay to their parent (on Mother's Day or Father's Day) or to their caretaker.

Ho, Minfong (1991). *The Clay Marble*. New York: Farrar, Straus & Giroux.

Heritage: Cambodian

Family Context:

✦ death in the family

✦ extended family

✦ family adversity

✦ family crisis

Genre: historical fiction

Grades: 6–8

This powerful novel is set in a refugee camp along the border of Cambodia. Twelve-year-old Dara is a refugee, as are her mother and brother. They are soon befriended by another fragmented family, which includes Jantu, a young girl about Dara's age. Brave Jantu shows Dara how to be independent and believe in herself. The two become very close as they endure a number of hardships together. Dara's newfound strength is severely tested when Jantu dies. However, Dara overcomes her grief and leads her new extended family back home in time to plant rice. The characters in this book are exceptionally vivid and three-dimensional, helping the reader feel the loss when Jantu dies.

Discussion and Beyond: Being Sensitive to the Losses of Others

Although the story dwells on the exceptional courage of Dara, the novel's portrayal of the extreme pain of all family members is deeply moving. Encourage students to brainstorm conversations that might be helpful to have with a youngster who has just experienced the loss of a family member.

Target Activity: A Letter to Dara

Have students write a letter to Dara expressing their sympathy over the death of her friend and the earlier loss of her family members. Encourage students to include words of hope and optimism about Dara's life with her new extended family.

Woodruff, Elvira (1992). *The Secret Funeral of Slim Jim the Snake.* **New York: Holiday House.**

Heritage: European

Family Context:
+ death in the family
+ aunt-nephew relationship
+ uncle-nephew relationship
+ family conflicts
+ family traditions

Genre: contemporary realistic fiction

Grades: 4–5

After his parents are killed in an automobile accident, ten-year-old Nick, who dreams of how life might have been with his parents, lives with his aunt and uncle above a funeral home. His uncle is a perfectionist who drives Nick crazy, a somber thread in the story. Humorous events also occur—one of them being a funeral for a snake, an affair that leads to a satisfying ending for the novel.

Discussion and Beyond: Accepting Difficult Family Transitions

With students, discuss the concerns that Nick might have had when he moved to a new home with his aunt and uncle. Discuss Nick's new situation and how he might have helped make the situation more acceptable. Ask students, working in small discussion groups, to answer the following questions:

1. Do you know any acquaintance who has lived with someone other than their biological parents? What was their situation? How did the situation differ from Nick's?

2. What changed when Nick moved in with his aunt and uncle?

3. If you had known Nick and his aunt and uncle during this time, what would you have done to help Nick when he said that his uncle was a perfectionist and was driving him crazy?

4. If you had known Nick during this time, what would you have said to him as he pursued his dreams of "what could have been" and "what if"?

Target Activity:
Recalling Humorous Family Events

Humor often made Nick's dysfunctional family life bearable, as so often happens in families. Using the family story of the funeral for a snake as an example, ask students to write about a humorous event that occurred in their family that either they experienced or that they heard about from other family members. Have them memorize their story and tell it to small student audiences.

Wyman, Andrea (1991). *Red Sky at Morning*. New York: Holiday House.

Heritage: European

Family Context:

✦ death in the family

✦ family adversity

✦ intergenerational relationship

Genre: historical fiction

Grades: 5–6

Twelve-year-old Callie Common shares the hardships experienced by her Indiana farm family in 1909. After Callie's mother dies, her father goes to Oregon, her sister leaves home to take a job, and she and her grandfather are left to work the farm in the midst of a diphtheria epidemic. After refusing to allow her grandfather to get close to her for many weeks, Callie begins to appreciate and love him as they work side by side on their farm and in the community.

Discussion and Beyond:
Families in Hardship

Ask the students to get any and all information they can about the chores of farm families who lived during the early twentieth century. Ask the students to discuss what it would be like to live during these times and whether or not they would like to live on a farm. Ask the students if they would like to work as twelve-year-old Callie Common did, on the family farm to help the family survive their economic hardships. Ask students if they have any suggestions for dividing the farm chores between Callie and her grandfather, and suggestions about how to combat a disease epidemic, if they were in a situation similar to Callie's.

Target Activity:
Managing Without a Parent

Ask students how one can be strengthened by an experience. What is the difference between family members living together with a parent and the family arrangement that Callie and her sister shared? Ask the students what impressed them about family life during the early 1900s and what questions they have. Write their questions on the chalkboard. Invite students to research their questions.

Beatty, Patricia (1981). *Lupita Mañana.* **New York: Morrow.**

Heritage: Hispanic

Family Context:

✦ death in the family

✦ family adversity

✦ family support

Genre: contemporary realistic fiction

Grades: 6–8

This story presents a moving and personal view of the illegal immigrant situation in the United States, bringing to light the pain and heartache of being an illegal immigrant in a most memorable way. When her father suddenly dies, thirteen-year-old Lupita emigrates from Mexico to the United States illegally. In slum alleyways, under the cover of night, in freight cars, and across the desert, gritty Lupita—dressed as a boy—learns the meaning of courage. The immigration police, who are forever on her trail, haunt her thoughts day and night. This book effectively portrays the plight of the illegal alien but also describes in realistic detail the plight of the poor family in the United States. The text is a poignant tribute to the courage and determination of young Lupita.

Discussion and Beyond:
Poor Families Can Be Rich in Love

Review the facts of poverty that were the reality of Lupita's life, and that are the reality of the lives of many illegal immigrants in America today. The stark reality of poor families—all over the world—is presented in this tribute to courage, determination, and family commitment. Ask students to recall how Lupita felt about her father and her mother. Do poor families love one another just as much as wealthier families do? Why?

Target Activity: A Rich Family

After the above discussion, invite the students to write a paragraph describing how a family without any material wealth could be considered "rich." Encourage students to support their paragraphs with illustrations, drawn or cut from magazines, that portray families engaged in loving and supportive activities. Arrange the paragraphs on the class bulletin board under the heading "Rich Families."

Lattimore, Deborah Nourse (1987). *The Flame of Peace: A Tale of the Aztecs.* **New York: Harper & Row.**

Heritage: Hispanic/Aztecan

Family Context:

✦ death in the family

✦ family heritage

✦ father-son relationship

Genre: folk literature

Grades: 4–8

In a story that borrows from the myths of the Aztecs, young Two Flint honors his father's death by going on a quest to bring a new flame of peace from the hill of Lord Morning Star. Along the way, he outwits nine demons, including Lord Smoking Mirror, who wears a cloak of forgetfulness, and the chattering bones of Lord and Lady Death. He is rewarded by Lord Morning Star with a "feathery touch" of New Fire, which he delivers to the temple in Tenochtitlan. There Two Flint glows "bright and true" to mark an end to war and fighting.

Discussion and Beyond:
Honoring a Family Member

Discuss the quest undertaken in honor of his father. Two Flint is rewarded for his persistence with fire. To further appreciate the idea of Two Flint honoring his father's death, have students offer suggestions about the part that fathers played in the Aztec culture.

Target Activity:
Honoring a Person's Memory

Ask students what is meant by the phrase "to honor someone's memory." Have students select a famous person (e.g., Washington; Lincoln; Martin Luther King, Jr.; etc.) for whom this country has created a national holiday. Have them write a simulated memorial speech explaining how schools, communities, and the media help the people of our country honor the person's memory. For those students who have dealt with the death of a grandparent or other family member, invite them to describe how they would like to honor that family member's memory.

Goble, Paul, reteller (1989). *Beyond the Ridge.* **Illustrated by Paul Goble. New York: Bradbury Press.**

Heritage: Native American

Family Context:

✦ death in the family

✦ family traditions

✦ intergenerational relationship

Genre: folk literature

Grades: 4–6

An elderly Native American grandmother goes from her deathbed to the world "beyond the ridge," pulls back to the world where her family mourns her, and then goes forward to where she is reunited with all her loved ones who have gone before her. The book includes Native American chants and prayers, and the illustrations contrast the sorrow and pain of the grieving family with the joy of the elderly grandmother as she travels beyond the ridge. The Native American perception of passing from life to death—only a change of worlds—presents a positive vision of life's cycle.

Discussion and Beyond: The Strength of the Elderly as They Pass from Life to Death

With the students, discuss this story and the strength of the elderly Native American grandmother. Read aloud some of the Native American chants and prayers, and discuss the words or phrases that express the need for a family member from any culture to be strong when facing death.

Target Activity: Death in Other Cultures

Have students select a culture, preferably that of their ancestors. Using encyclopedias, trade books, videos, and other resource materials suggested by the school or district library media specialist, have students research the culture's traditions regarding death. Have students write reports, concluding with personal reflection on how these traditions could help their family members cope with the death of a loved one.

Miles, Miska (1971). *Annie and the Old One.* **Illustrated by Peter Parnall. Boston: Little, Brown.**

Heritage: Native American

Family Context:

+ death in the family
+ family heritage
+ intergenerational relationship

Genre: contemporary realistic fiction

Grades: 4–6

In contemporary times of the 1970s, Annie cannot accept her grandmother's approaching death, which is related to the completion of the rug Grandmother is making. Annie tries to delay the completion of the rug by unraveling it each night, an act her grandmother discovers. Her grandmother takes Annie to a small mesa and talks with her: "This cannot be done . . . The sun comes up from the edge of earth in the morning. It returns to the edge of earth in the evening. Earth, from which good things come for the living creatures on it. Earth, to which all creatures finally go." Annie finally understands and returns to the hogan to help with the weaving.

Discussion and Beyond: Facing Death in a Family

Ask students why Annie was deliberately unraveling the rug instead of completing it. Did family members understand her behavior or become angry? Why? How did Annie's grandmother help her face her impending death? Why was this helpful to Annie? How do adults in American culture help young people prepare for the death of a loved one? How are young people in other cultures prepared for the death of a loved one?

Target Activity: Grandmother-Granddaughter Talks Together

Ask students to form partnerships to share anecdotal stories. Encourage them to tell each other family anecdotes in which an elderly family member talked with them and explained something to them, just as Annie's grandmother talked to her seriously about all creatures returning to Earth.

O'Dell, Scott, and Elizabeth Hall (1992). *Thunder Rolling in the Mountains.* **Boston: Houghton Mifflin.**

Heritage: Native American

Family Context:

✦ death in the family

✦ family adversity

✦ family support

Genre: historical fiction

Grades: 6–8

This narrative of displacement tells the story of the horrible winter of 1877, when the Nez Perce Nation of the Wallowa Valley in Oregon fled from the United States Army troops who were forcing them to move to a reservation in Montana. It is based on the recollections of survivors and some accounts of eyewitnesses. Sound of Running Feet, a Nez Perce Indian and daughter of the pacifist chief, is the narrator who describes the hardships of their flight, the deaths of some of her family members, and her decision to leave her father and escape to Canada rather than surrender to the troops.

Discussion and Beyond:
Facing Hardships with a Family

Ask students to compare the hardships of Sound of Running Feet with any hardships they and their family have encountered. What qualities must families have to face hardships of this magnitude and still survive? Why do hardships sometimes make a family stronger and bring them closer together?

Target Activity:
Pacifists and Their Families

Discuss with students the meaning of the term *pacifist*. Ask students why the chief of the Nez Perce chose to lead his people in flight—a pacifist stance—rather than in defending their land. Ask students to research the philosophies of two other famous pacifists, Martin Luther King, Jr. and Mahatma Ghandi. From their research, have them make a presentation to the class about why these men embraced a pacifist ideology. As a class, have students brainstorm situations in which it would be better to take a pacifist stance than to fight.

Nixon, Joan Lowery (1989). *A Place to Belong.* **New York: Bantam.**

Heritage: European

Family Context:

✦ death in the family

✦ family adversity

Genre: historical fiction

Grades: 4–6

Ten-year-old Danny and seven-year-old Peg are placed with Alfrid and Olga Swenson after their father dies. People in the Missouri Territory are divided over the issue of slavery, and Danny is teased about his and Alfrid's pro-abolitionist point of view. Eventually, Olga dies, but Alfrid remains a strong father figure. Later, Danny suggests that Alfrid send for his mother (hoping his mother will marry Alfrid). Mrs. Kelly, Danny and Peg's mother, arrives but falls in love with John Murphy, an Irishman. The entire Kelly family reunites at the marriage.

Discussion and Beyond: Benefits of a Remarriage in the Family

Ask the students to choose a class member to talk with about family situations in which a remarriage had several benefits. How were things better?

Target Activity: Family Reunions

As so often happens in families, the Kelly family forgot their differences and came together in love and support for the remarriage. Ask students to think of a time when their family came together in a spirit of love and support. Brainstorm possible occasions when this might happen (e.g., family reunion, birth of a new baby, christening, Bar Mitzvah or Bat Mitzvah, engagement party, wedding, graduation, hospitalization of a loved one, memorial or funeral service, etc.). Have students write a paragraph about the caring behavior of extended family members at the event they have chosen.

Appendix

Numbers indicate the page number where the annotation occurs.

Ethnic Backgrounds

Genres

Grades: 6+

Grades: 7–8

Grades: 7+

Grades: 8+

Themes

Absent Family Members

Absent Father

Absent Mother

Abusive Parent

Adopted Child/Adoptive Family

Adoption

Adoption/New Family

Alcoholism

Aunt-Nephew Relationship

Aunt-Niece Relationship

Community as Family

Physically Disabled Family Member
(Continued)

Sibling Relationship

Single Father

Single Mother

Stepfamilies

Two-Parent Family

Uncle-Nephew Relationship

Uncle-Niece Relationship

From # Teacher Ideas Press

EXPLORING DIVERSITY: Literature Themes and Activities for Grades 4–8
Jean E. Brown and Elaine C. Stephens

Take the riches of multicultural literature beyond the printed page and into the classroom. With a variety of themes, discussion questions, and activities that challenge misconceptions and stereotypes, this book gives students the opportunity to develop an understanding of and an appreciation for their own and other cultures. **Grades 4–8.**
x, 210p. 8½x11 paper ISBN 1-56308-322-1

LIVES OF PROMISE: Studies in Biography and Family History
Jerry D. Flack

Building on young people's natural curiosity about others, Flack guides students through the steps of researching and writing a biography or autobiography, offering a diversity of delightful, educational activities that invite youngsters to explore their history with such tools as maps, photo albums, and address books. **All Levels.**
x, 177p. 8½x11 paper ISBN 1-56308-045-1

THE PERSONA BOOK: Curriculum-Based Enrichment for Educators
Katherine Grimes Lallier and Nancy Robinson Marino

Watch class interest increase as your students "become" literary or historical figures, participating in events as the people they have chosen and creating projects based on their characters' lives. This book describes the concept of persona-based enrichment and offers five complete units. **Grades 4–7.**
x, 193p. 8½x11 paper ISBN 1-56308-443-0

U.S. HISTORY THROUGH CHILDREN'S LITERATURE:
From the Colonial Period to World War II
Wanda J. Miller

Enhance the study of U.S. history with historical fiction and nonfiction. Stepping back in time to experience a character's dilemmas, thoughts, feelings, and actions helps students easily grasp and retain a true understanding of an era. All the material you need to begin a literature-based history program is here. **Grades 4–8.**
xiv, 229p. 8½x11 paper ISBN 1-56308-440-6

WRITING THROUGH CHILDREN'S AND YOUNG ADULT LITERATURE, GRADES 4–8:
From Authors to Authorship
Mary Strong and Mimi Neamen

This acclaimed book uses students' natural responses to literature to guide them into creative action. It teaches the writing process naturally, using published works as the basis for writing experiences. Literature-based writing ideas, examples of students' writing, and vignettes that describe students at work on different projects are included. **Grades 4–8.**
xi, 173p. 8½x11 paper ISBN 1-56308-038-9

For a FREE catalog or to place an order, please contact:

Teacher Ideas Press
Dept. B60 · P.O. Box 6633 · Englewood, CO 80155-6633
1-800-237-6124, ext. 1 · Fax: 303-220-8843 · E-mail: lu-books@lu.com

Check out the TIP Web site!
www.lu.com/tip

9 781563 083136